Welcome

Tracing your family history has never been easier. With more and more documents going online, the door has been opened to anyone who wants to trace their family's past. Although what you see in an hour's episode of *Who Do You Think You Are?* has often taken months to research, there is no reason why you can't also give yourself the *Who Do You Think You Are?* treatment and uncover real stories of heroes and villains (as well as the ordinary folk, just trying to make a living) in your own family tree.

We have put together a series of articles that will help you on your quest, many of them written by researchers who work on *Who Do You Think You Are?* and all of them experts in their field. We have started with 20 simple steps that should set you on your road of discovery, followed by more in-depth articles that will help you overcome any stumbling blocks and take your research further.

Family history is an enthralling and life-enriching hobby that anybody can enjoy. This guide will help you set off in the right direction, guide you past the most common pitfalls and help you make the most of what is available online. It will be your guide as you discover your own *Who Do You Think You Are?* story. If you get stuck, or want to share any of your discoveries with others, come onto our forum where you are always welcome at ***www.whodoyouthinkyouare magazine.com***.

Happy hunting!

Sarah Williams, Editor
sarah.j.williams@immediate.co.uk

IMMEDIATE MEDIA CO

Who Do You Think You Are? Magazine
is published by Immediate Media Company
Bristol Limited

EDITORIAL
Managing editor Paul McGuinness
Editor Sarah Williams
Production editor Nige Tassell
Art editor Sheu-Kuie Ho
Picture editor James Cutmore
Contributors Robbie Bennie, Claire Vaughan, Matt Elton

ADVERTISING & MARKETING
Advertising director Caroline Herbert
Senior advertising manager Laura Gibbs
Advertising manager Hayley Smith
Account manager Sam Jones 0117 314 8847
Marketing executive Georgina Pearson

PRESS AND PUBLIC RELATIONS
Press officer Carolyn Wray 0117 314 8812
carolyn.wray@immediate.co.uk

LICENSING & SYNDICATION
Head of Licensing & Syndication
Joanna Alexandre +44 (0) 7150 5172

PRODUCTION
Production director Sarah Powell
Production co-ordinator Derrick Andrews
Ad co-ordinator Maria Stanford
Reprographics Tony Hunt and Chris Sutch

IMMEDIATE MEDIA COMPANY
Publishing director Andy Healy
Managing director Andy Marshall
CEO Tom Bureau
Deputy Chairman Peter Phippen
Chairman Stephen Alexander

SUBSCRIPTIONS AND BACK ISSUES
☎ 0844 844 0939,
✉ wdytya@servicehelpline.co.uk
or write to *Who Do You Think You Are? Magazine*, PO Box 279, Sittingbourne, Kent ME9 8DF.
Those with impaired hearing can call Minicom 01795 414561
Basic annual subscription rates:
UK £64.87, Eire & Europe £65, ROW £75

WALL TO WALL MEDIA LTD
Who Do You Think You Are? Magazine is produced under licence from Wall to Wall Media Ltd. Wall to Wall Media Ltd is part of Shed Media, PLC and is one of the world's leading producers of factual and drama programming. Wall to Wall is the producer of the multi-award winning television series *Who Do You Think You Are?* The series is committed to reducing its carbon emissions and has signed up to 10:10 (www.1010global.org). This has involved hiring more local crews and taking fewer flights while continuing to make a series that goes to wherever the story leads. Visit www.walltowall.co.uk for more information.

© Immediate Media Ltd 2014
Printed by William Gibbons Ltd.

Immediate Media Company Limited is working to ensure that all of its paper is sourced from well-managed forests.

This magazine can be recycled, for use in newspapers and packaging. Please remove any gifts, samples or wrapping and dispose of it at your local collection point.

THE ESSENTIAL GUIDE TO FAMILY HISTORY

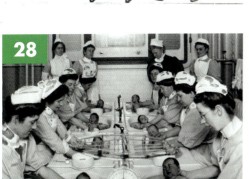

Contents

20 SIMPLE STEPS

The first 20 steps to start your family tree	6

BIRTHS, MARRIAGES & DEATHS

10 FAQs for tracking down lost births	28
Find that marriage!	38
How to date old family wedding photos	44
Records of death	48

CENSUS

How to use the census to find your ancestors	56

OUT AND ABOUT

50 hidden gems around the British Isles	67
London: Pin your capital ancestors down	74
Focus on Wales	80
Focus on Edinburgh	84
Focus on Dublin	88

OCCUPATIONS

Butcher, baker, candlestick maker?	92
Researching the Merchant Navy	98
Royal Navy ancestors	102
Find British Army records	106

SUBSCRIPTION OFFER

Subscribe to the UK's bestselling family history magazine	110

DIRECTORY

Selected online resources to help you in your research	112

Who Do You Think You Are? 5

20 SIMPLE STEPS
TO START YOUR FAMILY TREE

20 SIMPLE STEPS

TO START YOUR FAMILY TREE

STEP 1

Start with yourself

It sounds obvious, but you are the first entry on your tree

The golden rule of family history research is to start with what you know, so you won't be surprised to hear that it's you who is destined to be the first entry on your family tree.

Start by thinking about yourself and write down some of your key details. For example, when and where were you born? Who are your parents? Do you have siblings, a spouse or children? Sketching out a rough family tree is a good way to begin. Fill in as much information as you can about your parents, and – if you can – your grandparents and earlier generations. Write down all of the names, dates of birth, marriage and death, occupations, locations and any other information that you can remember about earlier generations of your family.

It's fine to put question marks or leave blanks if you're not sure about certain facts. You may find that you remember a birthday without being sure of the year, or that you recall a name without knowing whether it was their first name, middle name or nickname. Write it down anyway – there's time to find out for certain later. It is helpful to record whether you ever met these relations, and what they were like – their loves and hates, hobbies, appearance, personalities and anything else that you can remember.

Once you have retrieved everything you can from memory, it's time to go in search of useful documents that you may have about yourself and your ancestors. Perhaps you can find birth or marriage certificates, passports, awards, newspaper cuttings and photographs? There may even be a suitcase in the attic or a box under the bed containing such family memorabilia, which somebody else has collected, all providing clues as to who was doing what and when.

If you are extra lucky, you might find a family Bible recording several generations of your family, or a tree drawn by an ancestor, which takes the family back further than you are able. Now is the time to dust off these neglected gems.

You may find out what your ancestors looked like, what their handwriting was like and all kinds of other information that will leave you hungry for more. ∎

5 golden rules of family research

1 Begin with all the known facts and work backwards, checking the validity of each new piece of information against an original record.

2 Document your sources at each stage, whether that's a person or a piece of paper.

3 Keep a record of your research even if the avenue in question proves to be fruitless – it will stop you pursuing the same line of enquiry again at a later stage.

4 Do your own research. Don't assume that information that has been supplied to you by another party is accurate, and always check the authenticity of the information you find online.

5 When you hit a brick wall, you can often get help from family history societies, professional organisations and specialist magazines – like Who Do You Think You Are? Magazine

How many of your family can you already identify?

GLOSSARY

BMDs Short-hand for births, marriages and deaths, usually used in the context of birth, marriage and death certificates.

CENSUS This population snapshot is taken once every ten years. Census returns from 1841-1911 are available for England, Wales and Scotland, and 1901 and 1911 for Ireland.

CIVIL REGISTRATION The system under which all BMDs are recorded.

STATUTORY REGISTERS The name given to BMD records in Scotland.

PARISH REGISTERS The record of baptisms, marriages and burials kept by the church, now usually found at local record offices.

GRO The General Register Office, which issues BMDs. There is a GRO or equivalent for England and Wales, Scotland, Ireland and Northern Ireland.

20 SIMPLE STEPS TO START YOUR FAMILY TREE

STEP 2

Contact family

Getting in touch with living relatives opens up many new avenues

You've done what brainstorming you can by yourself, so it's time to get other family members involved. Some relations will know things that you don't about the family, perhaps because they are older and remember ancestors that you never met, or knew them at a different stage in their lives; or because they grew up with different relatives and were present at conversations when precious nuggets of information were revealed.

Email as many family members as you can and tell them what you are doing. Ask them if they have contact details of other family members you might not have. You may well find that somebody else within you family has already done some research that you can share. You may find someone who would like to get involved in the project. It's great to work with someone else. It not only reduces costs and effort, but it will help to inspire you and give you someone to share your discoveries with.

Of course, the people you really want to talk to are usually the older generation and they may not be on email. A letter or an initial phone call is a good start, but the very best thing you can do is arrange to meet up with them and interview them. Face-to-face interviews can produce more spontaneous memories than a request by letter or email. ■

Top tip!

If you don't get a response from your email, don't be disheartened. Follow it up with a phone call. People often think that the information they have is unimportant, but will be quite happy to answer questions over the phone.

Contact as many family members as you can – you never know what you might find

STEP 3

Interview relations

Try to record your family members' testimonies face to face...

Sometimes one family member is regarded as the guardian of the family history – someone who has photographs and memories and keeps in touch with more distant relatives. Decide who would be good to talk to, and then arrange a visit.

You should work your way round as many relatives as possible. You might even hold a small gathering where you can interview several relations in one day. For those who live further away, why not try emailing them questionnaires?

When you talk to family members, you should record the same kind of information that you did about yourself – names, dates and life details, as well as stories, characters, physical descriptions and anecdotes. It can be helpful to have a list of questions prepared – it is wonderful to let your relatives ramble and reminisce, but you don't want to get so caught up in their memories that you forget to ask some fundamental details.

Even if you manage to gather several members of the family together, it is helpful to interview each one separately, so that their memories do not become confused, and so everyone is able to speak freely without worrying about how others will respond to their information or stories. There may be disagreements about facts or events, and it is useful to record the various stories distinctly, rather than finding a confused compromise between the different versions. People are also often more open about information on a one-to-one basis.

Interviewing family members can be tremendous fun, but you may need to exercise a little tact and patience. ▷

A face-to-face interview can provide you with details you won't get from the archives

▷ Reminiscences may be long, rambling and contradictory, but let them flow. If your relatives are willing, you might record the interview – it would be a boon to future generations to have such footage of their ancestors! And remember to treat memories with respect. It may be amusing to you that your great great grandfather was a bigamist or appeared in court, but your grandmother is unlikely to take the same view.

Ask your relatives for any documents or photographs that they have hidden away. Photographs in particular can prompt memories, and it is often worth showing them to other family members, asking them to identify who is in them and letting the subsequent recollections flow.

Don't forget, memories aren't always entirely reliable, so check the facts with other family members and, if you can, against written documentation. ■

Dos and don'ts of interviewing relatives

✓ **Do** ask your relatives if anyone in the family has already done any genealogical research. They might be able to save you a lot of time.

✓ **Do** record the interview if you can – it will be a marvellous keepsake.

✓ **Do** take along family photographs to prompt memories. Ask your relatives to identify people and label them.

✓ **Do** treat memories with respect: you will be dealing with living memories, not mere history. What is funny or commonplace to you may be shameful or upsetting to someone of another generation.

✓ **Do** prepare a list of questions. You can get caught up in the stories and forget to ask for basic details.

✓ **Do** ask several relatives the same questions: you may be surprised by the variety of answers that you receive.

✓ **Do** follow up the interview with another meeting, letter, email or phone call. Once prompted, memories may slowly rise to the surface, so there may be more to come.

✓ **Do** write up your notes clearly, so you can easily find out who provided what information and when.

✗ **Don't** hurry your relative or bombard them with questions. Let them take their time, and allow memories to flow without interruption.

✗ **Don't** put words into your relatives' mouths. It is always better to ask, "what was your father like?" rather than the more leading, "your father was ambitious, wasn't he?".

✗ **Don't** press too hard for information that your relative is reluctant to divulge. You can ask again another time, but you don't want them to become uncomfortable and terminate the interview prematurely.

STEP 4

What do you want to achieve?

Planning in advance will save you time in the long run

You have written down what you know, you have contacted family members and hopefully spoken to some of them. You have sketched out a basic family tree. Now is the time to step back and decide where to go next.

Every generation you go back, your ancestors will double and you can't do everything at once. Is there a family story or mystery that you would like to get to the bottom of? Perhaps you feel that there is a particular branch of the family that you would like to know more about? You may just want to follow your family surname (although if you have a very common surname, you may be better off trying a different branch).

Set yourself a target and look at where the gaps in your knowledge are. This will help to give yourself a sense of direction and purpose in your research. ■

Working out a plan of action is important in order to keep you focussed on the task

20 SIMPLE STEPS TO START YOUR FAMILY TREE

STEP 5

Now get online

Most research is now done on the internet – so get online!

You have probably been keen to go online from the start, and now that you know some of the basics about your family tree, it's time to have an initial browse. You will be using the internet a lot during your research, either from home or at a library or record office.

It's amazing what you can find by simply entering the information you already know into a search engine such as Google. You might be able to find out more about your ancestor's profession, their town or village – or even pick up on a story about your ancestor themselves. This kind of searching is much easier if your ancestor had an unusual name.

This is also a great opportunity to see if someone else is researching your family (*see boxout below on Genes Reunited*) and to meet other family historians. Join the *Who Do You Think You Are? Magazine* forum (www.whodoyouthinkyouaremagazine.com/forum) or download the free app to meet other researchers who may be able to assist you.

Remember, you always need to check that any information you find online relates specifically to your ancestor, and not just to someone of the same name. Back up everything you find online with documentary evidence where possible or you could end up researching somebody else's family! ■

If you have an ancestor with an unusual name, try 'Googling' it and see what you get!

The *Who Do You Think You Are? Magazine* forum is a lively meeting place for family historians, from beginners to experts

Connect to other researchers through Genes Reunited

One way of linking up with people researching the same ancestor as yourself is to add your information to www.genesreunited.co.uk where other people upload their family trees. It lets you type in an ancestor and search other people's trees or add your own for free.

STEP 1:
Go to the Genes Reunited website and click on 'Register free'. Fill in your details and complete the necessary administration to register with the site.

STEP 2:
Enter the first name and surname of one of your ancestors in the 'Quick Search' box and click 'Search'. If you get too many results, you can add a year and place of birth.

STEP 3:
Click on 'Find out more' to contact the researcher who put the details of this ancestor online. You may find you have come across a new relative!

READ MORE: Turn to page 112 for a directory of useful online resources

STEP 6

Subscription websites

They may cost a little money, but these sites can pay dividends...

You may want to subscribe to a family history website. The big four subscription sites are: Ancestry.co.uk, findmypast.co.uk, GenesReunited.co.uk and TheGenealogist.co.uk. All offer England and Wales birth, marriage and death indexes, and England and Wales census records, 1841-1911. Ancestry.co.uk also covers the Scotland census up to 1901, but you'll need to visit ScotlandsPeople.gov.uk to see the actual images.

All four offer entry-level subscriptions that pretty much just offer those basic records, with prices ranging from £10.95 (for a month on Ancestry.co.uk), £19.95 (for a month's subscription to www.ukcensusonline.com, an entry-level offshoot of TheGenealogist.co.uk) to £69.95 (for six months on findmypast.co.uk). Most offer a free trial, so you can see which one suits you.

Once you go beyond the basics, the sites all have different records to offer, so it's really down to your requirements as to which one will be best for you. Some family historians subscribe to one website for one year and then try another one the next.

MONEY SAVING TIP
Most main libraries and record offices will offer free access to the Library Edition of Ancestry. Some now also offer free access to findmypast.co.uk.

Top tip!
Once you have chosen your subscription site, you can still visit any of the others if they have a specific dataset that may be of interest. Many offer a 'pay-as-you-go' option and some a free trial.

If your ancestors hailed from Scotland, then you will need to use ScotlandsPeople.gov.uk. This is a pay-as-you-go, rather than subscription, website but it has similar records to the other websites. ∎

---

5 value websites for family historians

Have a browse on these useful websites that are either completely free or at least free to search

www.thegazette.co.uk If your ancestor was awarded a medal, went bankrupt, changed their name, dissolved their business or engaged in any of the activities routinely recorded in the gazette, you are likely to find out more here.

www.nationalarchives.gov.uk/catalogue You may find your ancestors in military or legal records, divorce papers, naturalisation records, land records and more. You may need a trip to the archives in Kew to view any promising documents.

www.familysearch.org This massive genealogy site holds many and varied records and transcriptions from all over the world. Although the transcriptions are usually accurate, it is wise to obtain a copy of the original record if it is not available digitally on the site.

www.connectedhistories.org This portal site searches diverse sources – particularly from the capital – such as Old Bailey Online and the London Lives website. Although some sources need to be accessed via a library, there are plenty that are free.

www.britishnewspaperarchive.co.uk Although you have to pay to access the full stories (from £6.95 for up to 100 pages over two days), this vast archive is free to search, and covers newspapers from all over Britain. Your library may offer similar resources for free.

20 SIMPLE STEPS TO START YOUR FAMILY TREE

STEP 7

Start your family tree

Now is the time to start recording the fruits of your research

Begin to record your information systematically. Facts can become mixed up and take on a life of their own when they are not recorded carefully!

Some researchers like to draw their family trees by hand. Others download blank charts from the internet and fill them in as they go along. However, by far the most popular method now is to create a digital family tree that can easily be added to, shared and taken with you wherever you go. There are many excellent, easy-to-use software packages and online family tree builders available, which can make your life much easier when it comes to recording your information.

When deciding between an online family tree builder and family tree software, you need to be aware of the pros and cons of each. There are some great online family tree builders on the big four subscription websites, as well as at MyHeritage.com. These are accessible via the internet and can connect you to other researchers investigating the same ancestors as yourself. You may also be able to access your family tree from a smartphone using an app.

Before you begin, however, remember to read the small print to check that you are happy with how your data may be used. Some websites offer you the option of keeping your tree private if you prefer.

Although some online family tree builders offer many functions, there is nothing like good family tree software, especially when it comes to producing charts and storing large amounts of information about each ancestor.

Although the various packages have much in common, each has slightly different capabilities and system requirements. Look online to see what each one offers, and whether its approach will work for you. Check out reviews from other users. Most online family tree builders allow you to upload a GEDCOM (*see above*) exported from your software, so you can have the best of both worlds.

Each time you make a discovery, don't forget to enter it into your family tree. That way you won't lose track, and will be able to see more clearly what you need to do next. ■

> **GLOSSARY**
>
> **GEDCOM** This standard genealogy file format enables family historians to 'package' their family tree into a format that can be recognised by most family tree software and online family tree builders. If you build a digital family tree, you can usually 'export' it as a GEDCOM file and then 'import' it. The name itself comes from 'GEnealogical Data COMmunication'.

Online tree builders are a quick way to get started and share information

Six examples of family tree software

Family Historian 5
£36 PC
www.family-historian.co.uk
Packed with features, this is great for multimedia and charts. It produces GEDCOM-compatible files.

Family Tree Builder
Free PC
www.myheritage.com/family-tree-builder
This freebie has plenty of functionality but keeps things nice and simple with a series of wizards.

Family Tree Maker
£40/£60 PC or Mac
www.avanquest.com/uk
This popular option works seamlessly with Ancestry.co.uk – look for editions that come bundled with a trial subscription.

Heredis
£25/£37 PC and Mac
www.heredis.com
This software allows you to access your family tree from your Mac, iPhone, iPad or a PC. You can download a trial version for free.

MacFamilyTree 7
£30 Mac
www.syniumsoftware.com/macfamilytree
This program also has an app for integration into the FamilySearch.org online database.

RootsMagic 6
Free/£25 PC
www.rootsmagic.com
A decent all-round package that can run directly from a USB stick. A cut-down version – RootsMagic Essentials – is available for free.

STEP 8
Order a birth certificate
Confirm your research with official documents

Now that you've recorded what you know, and decided in which direction you want to go, it's time to start looking for documentary evidence of your ancestors.

Where you begin your search depends on the facts you already have. You need to be cautious about taking the names and dates provided by your family at face value. It's remarkable how easy it is to get the year wrong, or to refer to someone by a name that was not, in fact, their own.

It is always better to check – to order an extra certificate or two – than to take a risk and end up researching somebody else's family tree! ■

Pick a starting point
Decide where you have a really firm footing from which to start. If your family agrees about the name and birth date of your grandmother, but knows nothing about her parents, a good starting point would be her birth certificate. This will provide the names of both of her parents, enabling you to go back another generation.

Find the reference
To order this certificate, you'll need the relevant reference from the General Register Office (GRO) indexes. Log onto whichever subscription website you have chosen or try **FreeBMD.org.uk**, and search the England and Wales birth indexes. Birth indexes from 1911 will include the mother's maiden name.

Order from the GRO
Using the reference, order the certificate (for £9.25) from the GRO online, by telephone, or you can download an order form and do it by post (**www.gro.gov.uk/gro/content/certificates** for England and Wales). Now is the frustrating part – you will have to wait about a week for the certificate to arrive by post.

Check it's right
When the certificate arrives, check that the information recorded on it matches the facts you know to be true about your ancestor – their birthplace or the names of their parents. You will now have some new details to add to your family tree – in particular the names of two of your great grandparents. Another branch of your tree may start from a different footing. You might choose to research several branches simultaneously, or pursue one at a time.

Each birth certificate you can identify opens a number of new doors in your quest

Scottish birth certificates
Birth certificates in Scotland tend to be more detailed than in England and Wales. They usually contain a time as well as a date of birth, and the date of the parents' marriage. In 1855 they also included information about siblings and parents.
   Scottish birth certificates are indexed at **www.scotlandspeople.gov.uk** and, unlike for England and Wales, you can order a digital copy immediately for a small fee.

How to find missing birth certificates

If there are too many candidates
Reduce the options Try to narrow it down by comparing the district or area in the place of birth on the census with the districts for the candidates in the birth indexes. People did move about, but you might pick up some important clues.

Maiden names From the September quarter of 1911, the England and Wales birth indexes contain the mother's maiden name. This could reduce your options to one or two – and may also help you to spot siblings in the indexes.

Safety in numbers You may have to order more than one birth certificate to be sure you have the right one. This is much better than taking a chance and discovering months or years later that you got your facts wrong!

If there are no suitable candidates
21 again Try widening your search to include more years, as our ancestors were sometimes rather flexible about their ages.

Extra names Remember that girls in particular sometimes acquired a middle or Confirmation name between birth and marriage, and people sometimes changed the order of their names.

Sibling revelry If you cannot find a birth certificate, you might be able to locate one for a sibling from the census. This will provide you with the names of their parents.

Go to church If you can't find a birth certificate but know where an ancestor was born, search parish registers for their baptism.

READ MORE: Turn to page 36 to learn how to get the most from birth records

20 SIMPLE STEPS TO START YOUR FAMILY TREE

STEP 9

Order a marriage certificate

After the birth certificate, look for the marriage of the parents listed

You now know the names of your great grandparents, including the maiden name of your great grandmother, so it's time to search for their marriage certificate. The ceremony may have taken place about nine months before the birth of your grandmother, or she may have been the youngest in a long line of siblings, so you may have to search several years in the indexes to find what you're looking for. Of course, the marriage may also have taken place after the birth, although it should be evident on the birth certificate if the parents were not married.

Marriage references will appear in the civil registration indexes under the names of both bride and groom, with identical reference numbers. Most genealogical websites that host the General Register Office indexes, such as www.findmypast.co.uk, now allow you to match up the names to be confident that you have the correct entry. If you haven't yet signed up to a subscription site, try www.freebmd.org.uk.

Marriage certificates in England and Wales not only provide the names, ages, occupations, current marital status and residence of bride and groom, but the names and occupations of each of their fathers, too. Follow the same process as to order a birth certificate (*opposite*) when you come to order a marriage certificate.

When your certificate arrives, you will have the names of two of your great great grandfathers. The ages of the bride and groom will enable you to search for birth certificates for each, and the place of marriage may help narrow down the options in the birth indexes: note that it was traditional for a couple to marry in the bride's parish. The names and occupations of the fathers provide checking points so, when they arrive, you can verify that these birth certificates are correct.

You will now be able to continue ordering birth and marriage certificates, hopefully for generation after generation.

If the certificate doesn't quite ring true – perhaps the father's occupation is vastly different than expected, for instance – you may need to see if there are other possible options and order more than one certificate in order to be sure you have the correct one. ■

MONEY SAVING TIP
If you know where your ancestor married, check if the area's parish records are online – the information will be the same but cheaper, or maybe even free!

Marriage certificates contain a number of clues to continue your family tree

Scottish records

As with birth certificates, Scottish marriage certificates contain more detail than their English and Welsh equivalents as they name both parents of each spouse, including the maiden names of the mothers.

The first year of Scottish civil registration, 1855, was a great year for family historians: marriage certificates recorded the birthplace of bride and groom, and details about former marriages and the resulting children.

Scottish marriage certificates 1855-2006 (including many overseas) are indexed online at www.scotlandspeople.gov.uk.

Anyone researching Scottish ancestry is lucky because digital copies of the certificates from 1855-1935 are available instantly for a small fee from www.scotlandspeople.gov.uk.

Finding missing marriages

Often the correct marriage reference does not leap out of the indexes in the way we might wish. Here are some tips if you are struggling to find a certificate:

All change
Sometimes middle names were dropped or acquired between registration on a birth and marriage certificate, so extend your search accordingly. Or a child might adopt the surname of a step-parent or father-figure in preference to their birth name.

Alternative spellings
Spellings sometimes varied, so check for alternatives. Some websites include similar names in the results, or wildcard searches, where an asterisk replaces one or more letters, so entering Nichol* will produce results for Nichol, Nicholl, Nichols, Nicholson and so on.

Try parish records
If your ancestors are nowhere to be found in civil registration indexes but you know the area in which they married, you might substitute a parish record for the civil registration certificate. This should contain the same information.

READ MORE: learn how to get the most from marriage records on page 46

STEP 10

Consult the census

Census returns are a genealogical staple

Now that you have filled in a few 'holes' in your family tree, it's time to access one of the most useful sources in family history research. A census is a snapshot of a population. It aims to list every person, household by household, street by street, according to where they spent a single, specified night known as 'census night' – whether they were at home with their family, visiting friends, at boarding school, in hospital, in prison or anywhere else.

And it's not only names that are listed. Age, marital status, relationship to the head of the household, occupation, place of birth and, of course, where they spent the census night are the staples of genealogical research.

This kind of information feeds a family tree. The census is taken on one night every 10 years, and the returns for England, Wales and Scotland 1841-1911 and Ireland 1901 and 1911 are available to search online, either from one of the main subscription websites or from your local library.

Use your ancestor's birth certificate as your basis for searching the census. The information on the certificate – the names of the child and its parents, the place of birth and the occupation of the father – should enable you to identify the family on the first census after the birth.

It's great fun learning how to search a census, and although the search mechanism works slightly differently on the various websites, the basics are the same. Enter your ancestor's details, widening your search to include variations in name, age and place of birth if you don't strike gold straight away. Unfortunately, the information found on census returns is not always 100% accurate.

Not only were names, ages and spellings less rigidly important than they are today, but if a housewife believed (or wished) that she was 38 rather than 46, that would be the age recorded on the schedule. If her son William George was known as George in the family, then he will probably be George in the census. There was no check on the information.

The head of a large family has trouble remembering the names of his children on census day

Also, if a third party completed the schedule, they would record what they heard and make a stab at spelling unfamiliar names and places. If the enumerator or subsequent copyists could not read the handwriting, they too would have made a guess, as would those who eventually compiled the online indexes.

By understanding how the census was compiled, we are equipped to search for our ancestors with a flexible approach. With time and patience, you should be able to find your ancestors on every available census. ■

Find a person missing from the census

Searching for ancestors in the census can be tremendous fun. Sometimes they leap out at you from the indexes, other times considerable detective work is required to find the correct returns – which can be just as satisfying as an easy ride. If you are having trouble locating an ancestor, you might try some standard search techniques.

Less is more
Enter less information into the search box. For example, if you search for 'James Henry Mercer', and he recorded himself as 'James Mercer', you may overlook the correct entry.

Spell check
Spelling was more flexible in the past, and human error may also have crept in. If you are struggling to find William Cheek, try Cheak, Cheke or Check.

Happy families
Search for other members of the household. If you cannot find one ancestor, try searching for a family member that you would expect to find under the same roof.

Try before and after
If you are having trouble finding an ancestor on a particular census, pinpoint them on the censuses before and after and then try again. These will give you an idea of location, place of birth and so on.

Switch census sites
Try a different website with a different census index in case your ancestor's name has been misread by one indexer.

Address the problem
If you have an address for your ancestor, search for that (try www.findmypast.co.uk). A name may have been mis-indexed, but the house is likely to be there.

Still can't find your ancestor? It may be that they simply slipped through the net, or were recorded on a portion of the census that is missing. For instance, in 1861, Belgravia and Woolwich Arsenal sub-districts and some small parishes in Wales are not included. Missing returns are listed at www.findmypast.co.uk/helpadvice/knowledge-base/census/index.jsp.

READ MORE: Find out more about how the census can help you on page 56

20 SIMPLE STEPS TO START YOUR FAMILY TREE

STEP 11

Order a death certificate

Death records can provide vital information

We have already looked at collecting ancestors' birth and marriage certificates, and for family historians who just want to add names to their tree, those are the most important ones. But to get the complete picture of someone's life, you also need to know when and how they died.

A death certificate provides, among other details, the date, place and cause of death, the age of the deceased and the name of the informant. You will be able to see whether your ancestors died of an illness common to their era, or perhaps in an accident or some other unusual set of circumstances.

Often the duration of the last illness is recorded, enabling you to build a picture of the final days or years of their lives. You'll learn whether children were orphaned as a consequence, if family members died of the same cause and what kind of lifespans your ancestors had.

Obtaining a death certificate involves the same process as getting hold of a birth or marriage certificate (*see Step 8*). You will have to search for a reference in the indexes then order the certificate (for £9.25) and wait for it to arrive. Images of Scottish death certificates can be obtained instantly online from www.scotlandspeople.gov.uk.

You can often narrow down the period you need to search by looking at the census. For example, if your ancestor appears in 1891 but not on the 1901 census, it is likely that they died in the interim period – especially if their spouse is listed as widowed or has remarried by 1901.

In other cases, you may have to search from the last time you know your ancestor to have been alive until they would have been impossibly old. Note down all options from the indexes, then you can decide which is the most likely.

From 1866 onwards, the ages of the deceased appear in the indexes for England and Wales, making it easier to identify your ancestor. The registration district can also be compared with a location you know to be likely.

With a death certificate, you will know when and where your ancestor died. It may be worth checking local papers to see if an obituary was printed. Try and find out where they were buried in case further information is revealed on their gravestone (known as a memorial inscription). By the late 1800s most burials took place at civic burial grounds so records will be held by the local authority. Some have put them online at www.deceasedonline.com. ∎

Victorian mourning card

Scottish death and burial records

Civil registration began in Scotland in 1855 and the certificates contain more detail than English and Welsh equivalents. Scottish death certificates record the time as well as the date of death, marital status, name of the spouse (if relevant), duration of the last illness and the doctor who attended.

The names of both parents are recorded, including the mother's maiden name, helping researchers to be confident that they have correctly matched an individual's BMDs, as the same details are replicated on each.

Death certificates for 1855 also contain information about the birthplace and children of the deceased. Copies of the actual death certificates (1855-1958) can be viewed at www.scotlandspeople.gov.uk for a small fee.

Finding death records

- Remember that people sometimes adopted or dropped middle names, or may have varied the spellings of names, so broaden your searches of death records to allow for such eventualities.

- Your ancestor may have died away from home, either in a foreign country or elsewhere within the UK, so it is worth expanding your search accordingly.

- Members of the same family were often buried in the same plot or graveyard, even if it was a little distance from home. If you cannot find your ancestor in their home parish, have a look at other parishes associated with the family.

- Once you have located an ancestor's grave, monumental inscriptions can sometimes reveal further information, including the burial places of other relatives.

- Track down the relevant burial record for your ancestor – it could help you confirm their identity or find an elusive death certificate. Try www.deceasedonline.com.

Track down your ancestors' final resting place

READ MORE: Turn to page 54 to learn more about death certificates

STEP 12

Decide what to do next

With many avenues now open to you, where do you go next?

Should everything fall into place, statutory registration and the census will get your family tree back to 1837. Now is a good time for you to think about what you want to do next. Even if you answered the questions you initially had, you will no doubt have plenty more to keep you busy – there is always more to discover.

The next steps aren't necessarily chronological. If you want to go back further in time, then probably parish records will be your next port of call. If you have come across a soldier in the census records, then you may want to research some military records. An interesting occupation, such as coal-mining, might send you off down a different path.

You may prefer to concentrate on one individual and try to get as many records as possible about that person to build a picture of what their life was like.

Top tip!

Now's a great time to subscribe to *Who Do You Think You Are? Magazine* or book a ticket to *Who Do You Think You Are? live* in London in February 2014 for more inspiration and expert help.

STEP 13

Visit an archive

Get more from documents that aren't online

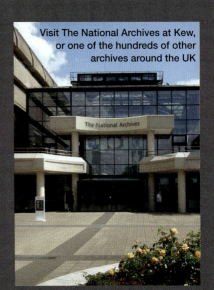

Visit The National Archives at Kew, or one of the hundreds of other archives around the UK

Although more and more content is going online, the information you can get through subscription websites and other online resources is just the tip of the iceberg. There will come a point in your research where you will really benefit from visiting an archive.

Those researching military ancestors should make a trip to The National Archives (TNA) at Kew, but a lot of records relevant to your ancestors will be held at the record office local to where they lived and worked. There is a very useful directory of archives, known as the ARCHON Directory, at www.nationalarchives.gov.uk/archon.

You can search what is available at archives in England and Wales using the Access to Archives catalogue at www.nationalarchives.gov.uk/a2a or try the National Register of Archives at www.nationalarchives.gov.uk/nra. If your forebears were Scots, you will need to visit the Scottish Archive Network at www.scan.org.uk.

It is always worth visiting the archive's own online catalogue as well, because these sometimes include more detailed and up-to-date information about holdings. When you arrive, feel free to ask for help from those who work at the archive.

5 tips for visiting an archive

1 Check the online catalogue and make a list of what you would like to see – it is easy to get distracted once you get there.

2 Contact the archive first if you are making a special or long journey and check the website for any special requirements.

3 Don't forget your digital camera as most archives will let you photograph documents – without a flash.

4 Bring your family tree with you as you may come across links you weren't expecting, which you will need to confirm.

5 Bring a pencil – some archives won't let you use pen – as well as food and drink if there isn't a café or shop close to hand.

20 SIMPLE STEPS TO START YOUR FAMILY TREE

STEP 14

Parish records

Trace your ancestors with church records

To trace ancestors back before 1837, parish records can prove invaluable

For events before civil registration (the official recording of births, marriages and deaths), parish records are a major resource. Civil registration began in England and Wales in 1837, in Scotland in 1855 and in Ireland in 1864 (where Protestant marriages were registered from 1845), but parish records of baptisms, marriages and burials can extend for centuries before this – the very earliest is from 1538.

These records work a bit differently to birth, marriage and death certificates. The information recorded is usually not as detailed. For example, ages and fathers' names do not routinely appear on marriage certificates and, without these checking points, it's difficult to be sure that the Elizabeth Smith who married in a parish in 1832 is the same Elizabeth Smith who was born there in 1809.

A census hit can provide clues as to time and place of birth for those who lived into the census era. But even if this helps you locate the correct baptism for Elizabeth Smith, this record will probably not reveal her mother's maiden name, so searching for her parents' marriage has a complication not found with civil registration.

If your family had an unusual name or remained in the same parish for generations, you will have an advantage when using parish records. If not, other sources may confirm your finds – wills are particularly useful for binding family members together and laying out exactly who is related to whom and how.

Parish records can usually be accessed free of charge in the relevant local or county archive. There are also some central repositories with large collections: examples include the Society of Genealogists (subscription or reading fee applies), the Family History Centres, run by the Church of Jesus Christ of Latter-Day Saints (LDS Church), and the National Library of Ireland. However, there are also great collections online, especially the LDS Church's free www.familysearch.org site.

Others appear on credits-based or subscription websites, such as www.ancestry.co.uk, www.scotlandspeople.gov.uk, www.findmypast.co.uk (which now boasts a vast collection of Welsh records) and www.thegenealogist.co.uk. Always check for online collections before you visit an archive. Essex Record Office has its parish registers online.

You may find nonconformists in your family – that is, people who did not attend mainstream church, such as Methodists, Quakers and Presbyterians. Records relating to these groups are available for a fee at www.bmdregisters.co.uk, www.thegenealogist.co.uk and www.ancestry.co.uk. ∎

Step-by-step guide to finding a baptism record

STEP 1:
Go to www.familysearch.org and enter the name of your forebear. Select 'Birth' beside 'Search by Life Events' and check 'Match all exactly' if you don't want too many results. Here we are searching for a George Smith, born in Cheshire about 1830.

STEP 2:
If you have too many options you can use the right-hand panel to refine your search or filter the results. We know about George because he appears on the 1851 census with his parents George and Margaret. You can click on 'Parents' and fill in their details.

STEP 3:
The results that come at the top are most likely to be your ancestor, although any that don't exactly match your terms are also included. Because the data in FamilySearch.org has come from many sources you may find more than one result matches.

STEP 4:
Click the name for more. In this case, there is no digitised image, but the transcript tells us George Smith was christened on 6 September 1832 at Wallasey in Cheshire, son of George Smith and Margaret. This is backed up by the Bishops Transcripts.

Who Do You Think You Are?

STEP 15
Military records

Uncover your ancestors' wartime experiences with these records

Many of us will have ancestors who were in the military at some time in their lives – either as soldiers, sailors or pilots. It may be that some military memorabilia survives in the family – perhaps medals, discharge papers, photographs or simply stories – which whet your appetite for further research.

There are plenty of records available to the family historian. Some of the most popular are First World War service records, War Diaries, army discharge papers, registers of seamen's services and campaign medal indexes, although this is just a fraction of what is on offer. It is helpful to remember when searching military records that there are often different sets of records for officers and other ranks, so make sure you are searching in the correct place.

Much of your ancestors' military history can be accessed cheaply and easily, although some may require you to visit an archive in person. The 40 per cent or so of First World War service records that survived bombing during the Second World War are available online at www.ancestry.co.uk, and you may be able to access this site for free at a local archive or library.

These records vary in their completeness and legibility, but may tell you the name and age of your ancestor, place of birth, previous occupation, next of kin, date of attestation, physical description, and information about regiment, service number, conduct, awards, wounds received and discharge. As you search these records, make sure you examine all of the options for the name you are interested in, and use details like next of kin and birthplace to pinpoint the right individual or dismiss other options.

Other collections of military records are also available online. For example, many of the records of soldiers discharged to pension before 1913 (TNA series WO 97) can be viewed at www.findmypast.co.uk. The Documents Online service at The National Archives (TNA) holds, among much else, Seamen's Service Records 1853-1923, First World War Campaign Medal Indexes and a selection of War Diaries.

The records can be downloaded for a small fee or accessed for free at TNA and other institutions. Records at TNA that are not online are often indexed online, so you can check these before embarking on a trip. TNA's website also hosts detailed research guides about tracing your military ancestors.

Your aim when using military records

Officers of the 1st Surrey Regiment, 1895

Tracing your ancestral war dead

It is often said that tracing ancestors who died in one of the world wars is easier than tracing those who survived.

One of the central resources for tracing war dead is the Commonwealth War Graves Commission, whose website (**www.cwgc.org**) is searchable for free, and contains information such as name, rank, regiment, service number, age, nationality, date of death and details of the grave reference and cemetery in which they were buried. There is often also information about next of kin and battalion, as well as plenty of background information (see *opposite*). You may end up making an ancestral pilgrimage to the resting place of your forebear.

Most military records from the Second World War are not yet available for the public to view. However, they can be released to the next of kin.

Visit **www.veterans-uk.info/service_records/army.html** for army records, **www.veterans-uk.info/service_records/royal_navy.html** for naval records and **www.veterans-uk.info/service_records/raf.html** for ancestors who served in the RAF.

20 SIMPLE STEPS
TO START YOUR FAMILY TREE

should be to pinpoint your ancestor as precisely as possible – for example, in terms of their rank, dates of service, which regiment they served with or vessels on which they served – then to research further to discover what this regiment or vessel did and when. This will therefore help to unlock what your ancestor's likely experiences would have been during their military career.

Regimental diaries can provide detailed and often harrowing information about what your ancestor was likely to have been doing at a particular time, although these records rarely mention individuals by name. ■

Might you have had an ancestor engaged at the Second Boer War, for example?

Military archives

The National Archives
www.nationalarchives.gov.uk
The National Archives are the major repository for military records in the UK.

Imperial War Museum
www.iwm.org.uk
Here you'll find all kinds of records, as well as a number of exhibitions and resources, which can help to put your ancestors' lives in context.

National Maritime Museum
www.nmm.ac.uk
This repository can supplement maritime records held at The National Archives but does not hold individual service records.

British Library: Asia, Pacific and Africa Collections
www.bl.uk
For records relating to those who served in British India and the Indian forces.

Regimental museums
www.armymuseums.org.uk
If you know your ancestor's regiment, contact the relevant museum, which should hold information about its campaigns.

National Army Museum
www.nam.ac.uk
Check out its online catalogue and visit the museum to find out more about army life.

Step-by-step guide to using the Commonwealth War Graves Commission website

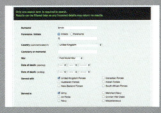

1 ACCESS THE SEARCH FACILITY
Go to the website at www.cwgc.org and either fill in the basics on the home page in the 'Search for Casualty' box, or click on 'Search for War Dead' in the red bar at the top for a more advanced search. This is best if your forebear had a common name.

2 FILL IN WHAT YOU KNOW
Fill in the details that you know – surname, initials, in which war they were killed, year of death, force and nationality. The more information you are sure of, the fewer false hits you will have. When you have completed the page, click on 'submit'.

3 LOCATE THE CORRECT RECORDS
Examine the options and match the information on each to what you know is correct about your ancestor. Clicking on a name will provide further details, helping you locate the correct entry.

4 FIND OUT ABOUT THE CEMETERY
Click on 'Find out more' by the name of the cemetery to discover further information, often including plans and photographs, about your ancestor's final resting place. There is plenty more to the site so make sure you have a good browse around.

READ MORE: More tips about ancestors in the military, starting on page 102

STEP 16

Occupation records

Work records can tell you a lot about your kin's day-to-day lives

During your research, you will come across many occupations listed in census records and on birth, marriage and death certificates. Many of these occupations will have generated a paper trail that might give you even more insight into the lives of your ancestors.

Even if you don't find direct records relating to your forebear, researching their occupation may still prove fascinating. Some employers, such as the Post Office, kept detailed records, many of which survive and can be easily accessed (some at Ancestry.co.uk, although even more are held at the Royal Mail archive). However, for many industries it can be hit and miss.

If you know the name of the company that your forebear worked for, then search the National Register of Archives at www.nationalarchives.gov.uk/nra or, if in Scotland, www.scan.org.uk. Records you may come across include trade and professional directories, apprenticeship records, trade union records, disciplinary books, staff registers, appointment and wages books, staff and union magazines, pensions, licenses and estate records.

You may need to check with the local record office to find out what might be available or search ARCHON (www.nationalarchives.gov.uk/archon) to see if there is a specialist archive. The Society of Genealogists (www.sog.org.uk) also has a lot of useful material on occupations including teacher registrations (now also available on www.findmypast.co.uk). ∎

4 specialist archives

Royal Mail Archive
🖥 www.postalheritage.org.uk
Although some of the Royal Mail Archive is now available at **Ancestry.co.uk**, it is worth visiting the archive to access further material.

Scottish Business Archive
🖥 www.gla.ac.uk/services/archives/collections/business
Holdings cover the whole of Scotland with occupations, including brewing and whisky production, shipping, railways and textiles.

Museum of English Rural Life
🖥 www.reading.ac.uk/merl
This museum's archive holds records from farms and agricultural firms, as well as some company archives, including those of Huntley and Palmer and Massey Ferguson.

National Waterways Museum
🖥 www.nwm.org.uk
If your ancestor worked on the canals, it is worth visiting this site to see if it might hold material relating to them or their work.

READ MORE: Turn to page 92 to learn more about occupational records ➤

STEP 17

Poor records

Ancestors who needed financial aid left a trail of records to follow

As any fan of the *Who Do You Think You Are?* television series will know, those of our ancestors who were unfortunate enough to find themselves penniless often left a trail of records.

The Poor Law Amendment Act of 1834 reformed the way poor relief was administered in much of the UK, with the exception of Scotland, which reformed its poor law in 1845.

Before 1834, poor relief was administered by the parish and usually consisted of 'outdoor relief', such as food, money, fuel or other forms of direct help. Under the new act,

Might these workhouse boys be your relatives?

20 SIMPLE STEPS
TO START YOUR FAMILY TREE

relief was administered by Poor Law Unions and was almost always in the form of the dreaded workhouse.

You may also find your ancestor mentioned in correspondence between the Poor Law Commission and the Unions. This can be partially searched on TNA's Discovery site (http://discovery.nationalarchives.gov.uk).

Where records survive, they can make for fascinating reading. Ask at the local record office for details of what has survived. If you do find an ancestor in the workhouse, then you should visit www.workhouses.org.uk. Some records of London workhouses are available online on at Ancestry.co.uk and www.londonlives.org. ∎

Scottish poor records

Prior to 1845, the funding and administration of poor relief in Scotland was shared by the kirk sessions (church authorities) and heritors (landowners) in each parish.

Support for the destitute was mostly through outdoor relief, although Edinburgh, Glasgow and some towns established poorhouses (the Scottish term for workhouses) to house the destitute.

Records include minute books and accounts of the heritors and kirk sessions that feature details of poor relief applications and payments. Other surviving documents may include parish poor's rolls – lists of named individuals receiving relief.

In 1845, the Poor Law Act (Scotland) introduced a new system of poor relief – from which the able-bodied were explicitly excluded. Although relief could still be given either in cash or in kind, large parishes and groups or 'combinations' of smaller parishes set up poorhouses.

Your ancestors' hardship could be your good fortune

Who Do You Think You Are? 23

STEP 18

Read all about it!

From weddings to obituaries, newspapers can be a goldmine....

Newspapers are a rich well of potential leads to discover more about your forebears

Warning
Don't assume that a story is about your ancestor just because you see their name in print. Even unusual names can be common in some areas. Always look for documentation to back up the story.

Newspapers have always been a fantastically rich resource for family historians, but in the past they were extremely time-consuming to use and you really had to know what you were looking for and when it happened.

Now that more and more newspapers are being digitised, this incredible resource is being opened up for speculative searching. This means that, instead of scrolling through pages and pages of microfilm at a record office, you can type in a few search terms and see what comes up. If you strike lucky then it could lead you to new lines of investigation.

As well as stories of crime, mishap, sporting achievement and bankruptcy, newspapers also announce births, marriages and deaths and could give you crucial information that will help you to order the correct certificate. If you are lucky, you may find an obituary of one of your ancestors that can reveal lots of personal details.

If you find an ancestor mentioned, it is worth checking other local newspapers to see if they also ran with the story. Something that only warrants a sentence in a major newspaper might run to a few paragraphs or more in a smaller or more local title.

The British Library is in the process of digitising the most used part of its newspaper collection and this can viewed online at www.britishnewspaperarchive.co.uk. Or visit the relevant local record office, which should have collections of old newspapers on microfilm. Some family history societies have produced name indexes for local newspapers.

MONEY SAVING TIP
If you are a member of your local library, you may be able to access *The Times* digital archive and the British Library's 19th-century newspapers website for free from home. Check with your library about remote access.

Newspaper resources

List of online newspaper archives
- http://en.wikipedia.org/wiki/Wikipedia:List_of_online_newspaper_archives
This page is invaluable for tracking down digital newspapers from around the world.

British Library
- www.bl.uk/welcome/newspapers.html
The British Library website leads you to the British Library's amazing online collections that can also be viewed at www.britishnewspaperarchive.co.uk.

Gazettes online
- www.thegazette.co.uk
The *London*, *Edinburgh* and *Belfast Gazettes* published insolvency notices, military awards and other public details – and it's free to search online.

***The Times* Digital Archive**
Ask your local library about access to *The Times* digital archive. Great for announcements of births, engagements, marriages and deaths.

Australian newspapers
- www.trove.nla.gov.au/newspaper
A fantastic free site if your forebears emigrated to Australia.

20 SIMPLE STEPS TO START YOUR FAMILY TREE

STEP 19

Take it further

Delve deeper into your family history, just like the professionals…

You are more than a beginner now! Once you have completed these first steps, you are on your way to truly getting the family history bug. You may use the resources mentioned here time and again but as your research progresses you will need to hunt down further documents to help you build your family tree.

There is plenty of help online for those who want to take their research further. For specific help with a problem, forums can really come in handy. Some specialist forums, such as the Great War Forum (www.1914-1918.invisionzone.com/forums), can be a boon for those who have hit a brick wall in their research and need some expert advice.

The *Who Do You Think You Are? Magazine* forum (wwwwhodoyouthinkyouaremagazine.com/forum) is a great place to share problems and is now available to download as an app. You may want to join a family history society. Visit www.ffhs.org.uk to find one that suits.

You should also consider a trip to the annual Who Do You Think You Are? Live show (www.whodoyouthinkyouarelive.com), which is held at Olympia in London in February. As the world's largest family history fair, it has something for everyone, with workshops, stands, celebrity talks and lots of expert help to hand.

Finally, subscribing to *Who Do You Think You Are? Magazine* will help you every month to discover useful records, learn new techniques and find out about the latest resources as soon as they come online. It won't take long before you feel more confident with your researching. You will probably even find yourself giving advice to others! ■

Get more from family history forums online

Forums are communities of like-minded people where you can post a question or answer somebody else's post. Here are some tips to help you get more from them.

Have a look at other people's posts first to familiarise yourself with the community.

Keep your query concise and include any information you have, so people don't waste time researching what you already know.

Remember to check back to see if anybody has responded and thank people for answers.

Avoid mentioning details of people who are still alive and don't include your email address publicly. Use private messages for this instead.

STEP 20

Share your family history

Don't keep your research to yourself – others may benefit from it!

Your family history is a story that has no ending, but at some point you will have gleaned enough information to put together something that is worth sharing with others. A simple email or letter at Christmas might prompt other family members to add to your research.

Many genealogists create their own websites to house the results of their research. Designing your ancestral website can be great fun and also makes it much easier for other interested parties to access your research without you having to send them lots of files or documents.

Alternatively, you might create a Facebook page (www.facebook.com) to keep your friends and relatives up-to-date with your finds, or use another social networking site to share information and photographs – try www.historypin.com or www.flickr.com. Or you could blog about your research. Blogs can be set up via www.blogster.com or www.blogger.com, among others.

When posting information about your genealogy online, remember to ask permission from your living relatives before putting any of their details on the web.

You may find that by putting your family history online you come across living relatives that you knew nothing about who are researching some of your forebears but on a different branch of their tree.

Finally, if you do uncover a good story, don't forget to share it with other family historians via *Who Do You Think You Are? Magazine*! ■

ONE EVENT ONE WEEKEND

Your opportunity to meet leading genealogy experts at the world's biggest family history show

WHO DO YOU THINK YOU ARE? LIVE
sponsored by ancestry.co.uk

Don't miss the chance to find your ancestors at Who Do You Think You Are? Live

Welcome to the world's biggest family history show where you'll find leading genealogists, specialist exhibitors, free workshops and celebrities from the television series all under one roof! Sponsored by Ancestry.co.uk, you'll find the help and advice from our experts you need to explore your family tree

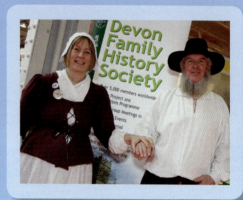
Find regional expertise from across the UK

Identify your military ancestors

Attend one of our informative workshops

TICKET OFFER
BUY TWO TICKETS FOR £26*
QUOTE CODE: WW2426

TO BOOK TICKETS*
CALL 0844 873 7330 OR VISIT:

www.whodoyouthinkyouarelive.co.uk

*£2.25 transaction fee applies. Usual ticket price £16. Two for £26 offer ends 14th February 2014

Please note, tickets to our workshops are free on the day on a first come, first serve basis. However, you can book up to two

ONE PLACE TO FIND YOUR FAMILY

THE WORLD'S BIGGEST FAMILY HISTORY EVENT

TICKET OFFER Buy 2 tickets for £26*

Enjoy a one-to-one session with an expert

Date your old family photos

Meet our exhibitors! We have over 150 specialist exhibitors and you'll find exclusive show discounts and special offers you won't find anywhere else

NEW! Military History Area commemorating WWI

OLYMPIA LONDON
THUR 20–SAT 22 FEBRUARY 2014

TICKET TYPES	ADV / ON DOOR
STANDARD TICKET	£16 / £22
TWO DAY	£26 / £26
THREE DAY	£33 / £33

BEGINNER TICKET £22
Price includes three pre-booked workshops, beginner's guides to the event, a tree planner, reserved seats in the Ancestry.co.uk Academy and a copy of WDYTYA? Magazine.

ANCESTRY VIP £28
Price includes fast track entry, three pre-booked workshops, a pre-booked Ask the Experts session, show guide & reserved seats at your selected SoG workshop and theatre sessions.

workshop tickets per entry ticket in advance, at a cost of £2 each, when purchasing your show ticket. Children under 16 go free.

Newborn babies being bathed in London, 1910

BIRTHS, MARRIAGES & DEATHS
RESEARCHING BIRTHS

10 FAQs for tracking down lost births

Birth records are one of the most valuable tools in the genealogist's arsenal. Family history expert **Jenny Thomas** answers the essential questions about this crucial resource for your research

Birth records are one of the most important resources available to genealogists. Time and again, they provide a treasure trove of information to feed a family tree. As you dig deeper into your family's past, you're likely to acquire dozens of birth records. Each one will enlighten you in one way or another.

So let's have a look at the major record sets that are available, what they have to offer and how to get hold of them – and how you might leap over some of the hurdles and avoid some of the pitfalls that the records and their indexes like to place in your path.

There are two major types of birth records championed by family historians: birth certificates and baptism records. Birth certificates were (and still are) documents produced by the state as part of the process of civil registration. From 1837 in England and Wales, 1855 in Scotland and 1864 in Ireland, the parents of a new-born baby were obliged to register the birth. The resulting certificate contains key information for your family tree: the full name of the child and its parents, including the mother's maiden name; the date and place of birth; the father's occupation; and the name of the informant. In Scotland, the date of the parents' marriage is also helpfully recorded for most years.

In order to access a birth certificate, family historians have to search the birth indexes to find a reference number for the certificate they want, which they can then purchase from the General Register Office. The indexes are available online – and arranged by quarter – so a typical birth reference might look like this:

**DAWSON Sarah Jane
April, May, June 1900
Plymouth 5b 230**

This means that the birth of Sarah Jane Dawson was registered in the June quarter of 1900 (in other words, in April, May or June; there are also March, September and December quarters) in the district of Plymouth. The reference number 5b 230 is needed to order the certificate, which you will have to do in order to view the full information it contains. Note that the indexes indicate in which quarter the birth was registered, which was supposed to be within six weeks of the birth, and not when the birth itself took place. This means that even if you know that your grandmother was born on 15 June, her birth may have been registered in July, and thus the reference will fall into the September quarter.

▷

Who Do You Think You Are? 29

▷ For the pre-civil registration era, baptism records are an essential resource. These can, in exceptional cases, get you back to 1538 in England and Wales, when the state reached out to seize greater control over the key events in people's lives and demanded the systemised recording of baptisms, marriages and burials in each parish. In Scotland and Ireland, the records rarely go back so far. Baptism registers were produced on a parish-by-parish basis and are now usually held at the relevant local record office or in national repositories, or both – although large collections are also available online.

Baptism records tend to contain less information than birth certificates. The name of the child, name of the father and date of baptism are fairly standard, and other information may also appear: the name of the mother, occupation or address of the father, date of birth and more. Remember that these records are of when the child was baptised, not when they were born, and there might be days, weeks, months or even years in between, so they cannot always be used to establish a precise age for your ancestor.

1. I can't find my ancestor in the birth indexes. What do I do now?

This is bound to happen to you at least once as you research your family tree. Now is the moment to become a true detective. First of all, widen your search parameters a little. Remember that our ancestors were not as rigid about spelling and age as we are today, so be a little generous in your chosen search terms. If you are looking for Louisa Pallett, try Louisa Palett, Palet and Pallet. Many genealogical websites contain the facility for wildcard, soundex and phonetic searches, allowing, in various ways, for alternative spellings, so take advantage of them. It's also a good idea to give your ancestor a margin of a couple of years when you calculate their year of birth.

Remember that they might have had reason to be economical with the truth on other documents in your possession. Perhaps someone wanted to appear old enough on their marriage certificate to marry without parental consent. Or a bride might doctor her age a little at marriage, so as to appear younger than the groom and perhaps maintain the pretence on future census returns. Although it's always a good idea to gather several census returns and other documents about your ancestor to guide you towards their birth record, it's also helpful to be aware of the potential pitfalls.

In rather more complicated scenarios, it may be that your ancestor was born under a different name to the one used on subsequent documentation. For example, if the eldest child or children in a family were born before the marriage of the parents, they should appear in the indexes under the mother's maiden name, even if they adopted the name of their real or stepfather between their birth and their marriage.

Check both birth certificates and baptism records to locate missing forebears

You might find that the information on a birth certificate is not what you were expecting

Watch out!
Don't dismiss a birth record because the information isn't what you expected, especially if you base your search on census information. Details are sometimes hidden on the census. The child you are researching might be an illegitimate grandchild. Or your ancestor's mother might have died between the birth and the census, and the father remarried, meaning that the certificate may, in fact, be right.

BIRTHS, MARRIAGES & DEATHS
RESEARCHING BIRTHS

Alternatively, your ancestor may have been born in an unexpected place. Although census returns may declare that great-uncle George was born in Liverpool, he may have thought it diplomatic to declare his place of residence as his birthplace, even though he had actually immigrated from Ireland. Once again, it's helpful to gather as many documents as you can for each ancestor and to take into account any variations in the information they provide.

2 There are loads of options for the birth certificate I want. Can I tell them apart?

This, too, is a common problem and sometimes requires considerable detective skills to resolve. There's no doubt that ancestors with unusual names make a genealogist's life easier and if you come across a William Smith or Jane Jones in your family tree, your task is likely to be more difficult. It's a good idea to make a full list of all options for the correct birth and then work to narrow them down. Have a close look at the place of birth on the census, compare them to the district in which the birth was registered and decide which are the most likely options. You might consider in which district other family members were born or died, or where they lived.

Alternatively, note where a female ancestor married, as it was traditional that a couple married in the bride's parish.

Alternatively, it may be that there is a sibling with a more unusual name who would be easier to find in the birth records: you will have a better time searching for Violet Felicity Brown than you will for her brother John Brown. But the bottom line remains that you may have to order more than one birth certificate to be sure you have the correct one. All possibilities should be examined, before being accepted or rejected for a good reason.

Ancestors with strange names make research much easier

Remember that very common names can lead to confusion even if you have the father's name from the marriage certificate as a checking point. For example, there may be several options in the birth indexes for a John Davies born in 1869 in Merthyr Tydfil – and more than one of these may have the same father's name, or even the same mother's name, too. So if you leap upon the first one that appears correct, you may be building on shaky ground. Precise addresses, occupations, the identity of siblings and all the detective skills you can muster become increasingly important in such circumstances.

3 My ancestor was illegitimate. How can I trace the father?

Sometimes on a birth certificate, the 'name of father' column is left blank. On a baptism record, an illegitimate child may be referred to as 'a bastard' or 'base-born', or simply have no father's name recorded. Without the father's name, one line of your family tree will, by necessity, close down, but there are sometimes ways of establishing, or at least surmising, the identity of the father.

Sometimes the father of your illegitimate ancestor will be the man the mother subsequently married, although it's difficult to tell whether this man was the biological father or simply a 'father figure' for the child. Occasionally, the child's name hints at the identity of the father: for example, a child may be given a distinctive first or middle name, which just happens to be shared by the lodger, the mother's employer or the man next door. Educated guesses are sometimes possible.

It's worth having a look at the child's baptism record, even if you have the birth certificate, as it may just say 'the reputed child' of so-and-so, giving you a clue.

A destitute mother on the way to the workhouse, 1754

▷ Bastardy examination records, which are usually held in the relevant local or county record office, are also worth a peek. This rather brutal interrogation was undertaken in the interests of the parish, which, as the provider of poor relief, had an interest in establishing the identity of the father of an illegitimate child in order to force him to support that child.

An illegitimate child might be provided for in a will, or you may find your illegitimate ancestor benefiting from a surprising level of education or wealth, or entering into a costly apprenticeship that arouses your suspicions and leads you to scour any relevant records.

Of course, none of these techniques for identifying a father is cast-iron: you cannot absolutely guarantee that you have identified the correct father. The mother might have married someone other than the father of her child; she might even have lied at her bastardy examination, simply picking on a man she knew was rich enough to support the child.

But it's worth noting that even when you do have a solid document trail, you can still never be utterly certain of your facts. How many fathers, for example, are present and correct on an ancestor's birth certificate when they were not in fact the father of the child?

4 What if the ancestor I am looking for was born abroad?

Often you will know either from the census or from family tales that one of your ancestors was born abroad, but this by no means spells the end of the trail. It is helpful to establish the place of birth as precisely as possible, which is often done by gathering as many census returns as you can. While the 1891 census may record 'India' or 'France' as the place of birth, 1901 might narrow it down to 'Calcutta' or 'Toulouse'.

For British subjects born overseas, indexes and certificates are available in the same way as domestic ones. There are indexes of British Nationals born overseas, or indeed at sea, and separate indexes of maritime and armed forces births. There is also a separate index of 'minor records' as Scottish births overseas are called, online. The discovery of ancestors born abroad inevitably leads to other interesting questions: what were the parents doing there? Were they there as part of the military, or involved in colonial administration or missionary work? Were they working there, on holiday, visiting family or in some other capacity?

If your ancestor was born abroad to a foreign family, and subsequently immigrated to the UK, their birth will not be registered here. However, the event is likely to have been registered in their country of origin; it is then a case of establishing as precise a location as you can and approaching the relevant local archives, who are likely to be able to point you in the right direction. If you're lucky, your ancestor may have become a naturalised British subject, and therefore their naturalisation papers, held at The National Archives, may give considerable detail about where they came from, who their parents were and other genealogically relevant information to help you on your way.

For ancestors born in British India, the British Library India Office holds many of the relevant records, and many have made their way online.

5 I've tried all your hints, but my ancestor simply isn't in the birth indexes. What are my options now?

Keep trying – just a little longer. Perhaps when the national indexes were compiled, your ancestor's name slipped through the net, even though they were correctly registered and a certificate produced. Have a look at local indexes. These indexes were copied and amalgamated into the national indexes that you search online, but there are bound to be some administrative errors. Inevitably, some individuals will appear locally who are nowhere to be seen nationally. Certificates

Records should be available for British subjects born abroad in the same way as had they been born in Britain

located in local indexes can be ordered from the relevant local register office: the reference number in these indexes will mean nothing in the General Register Office system.

In the end, however, there does come a time to admit defeat – a difficult thing for genealogists to say! Not all of our ancestors

It is possible that you may never find your missing ancestor

BIRTHS, MARRIAGES & DEATHS
RESEARCHING BIRTHS

had their births recorded as they should have done, whether their parents acted accidentally or deliberately. Not everyone recognised the importance of registering their child; others were fiercely resistant to the system, especially in the early decades.

Sometimes first-time parents did not manage to register their eldest child, but did so for subsequent children. The same is particularly true of new immigrants who did not know the system and who perhaps did not speak the language sufficiently to be able to negotiate it. So, if you really can't find the birth of the child you are interested in, why not have a look for a sibling?

The certificate will provide much of the essential information you need to continue building your tree, not least the full names of both parents. It's especially helpful if the sibling was born close to a census year; you can hopefully match their birth address with the address you know to be correct for your ancestor on the census.

Remember, too, that even if your ancestor does not appear in civil registration, they may well appear in parish records or in the records of their place of worship. These records continued to be kept during the period of civil registration and are well worth a look if you are having trouble elsewhere. ▷

CASE STUDY FROM THE SHOW
AMANDA REDMAN

Actress Amanda Redman had an exciting time tracing her St Ledger ancestors, who migrated to Cornwall from Ireland in the 1850s. Amanda's family had always believed that they came from a long line of Irish Protestants, a theory the records initially supported. At the Protestant St Mary's Church in New Ross, Amanda viewed the baptism record of her great great grandfather James St Ledger, who was born in January 1835 to John and Mary St Ledger of New Ross. John was employed as a servant. However, Amanda encountered an obstacle with the next generation back. Hoping to find a baptism record in the same parish for John St Ledger, she was only able to find a record of his Confirmation when he was a pupil at the local Charter School.

A meeting with an expert revealed that the Charter School was an institution for destitute or orphaned Protestant boys, but nevertheless a surprised Amanda was advised to search for John's baptism in Catholic records. She learned that a child was deemed to have better chances in life if they grew up Protestant, including attending the Charter School and gaining employment with Protestant English families. So Amanda visited the local Catholic church where she found the baptism of her 3x great grandfather, John St Ledger, in June 1812.

With her ancestors having started out as Catholics and later converting to Protestantism, Amanda discovered how useful it can be to search for baptism records in unexpected places.

Who Do You Think You Are?

A Quakers' meeting in London, 1736

6. I can't find my ancestor's baptism record anywhere. Where do I look next?

The majority of our ancestors were baptised in mainstream parish churches, but by no means all. If your ancestors do not appear in these records, it's a good idea to search for them in nonconformist records – for example, records of Baptist, Methodist, Quaker and Presbyterian churches, many of which are available online.

You may have no inkling that your ancestors were nonconformist, but this feature of their lives is more likely to be revealed through baptism records than anywhere else. Following Hardwicke's Marriage Act, 1753, all marriages (except those to Jewish and Quaker families) had to be performed by a Church of England clergyman, and so the marriages of your nonconformist ancestors would have had to take place in the mainstream parish church, and be recorded in mainstream parish records.

Similarly, many nonconformist congregations would not have had their own burial ground, so their members will have been buried along with everyone else in the parish graveyard and entered into the mainstream burial records accordingly. So baptism records are sometimes the only place you pick up the scent of your ancestors' nonconformity: they are well worth a check, both to enable you to continue building your family tree, and as an interesting piece of religious and social history in which your ancestors were involved.

7. How do I know which parish to search to find my ancestor's baptism record?

If only there were a simple answer! Once again, the census is a key resource – and you need to find as many returns as you can. While one may simply say that your ancestor was born in Ireland, another might provide the county, township or parish, which is a tremendous help. And, just as with civil registration, it's helpful to have a look at where other family members were born, married and died.

Many genealogists begin by searching the most likely parish – and then expand to neighbouring parishes and so on – until they strike gold. However, with large collections of parish records now available online, it's possible to search wide areas at the touch of a button. It is important, however, to know exactly what you have searched and what remains to be searched, either on another website or offline.

One candidate for the baptism record you want does not necessarily mean you have found the right one. Eliminating other options brings you one step closer to your goal. A particularly useful reference book for discovering the location and boundaries

BIRTHS, MARRIAGES & DEATHS
RESEARCHING BIRTHS

of parishes, and which records are available in England, Wales and Scotland, is *Phillimore's Atlas and Index of Parish Records*.

8 How do I know that the baptism I have found is correct?

This is another perennial question, one to which there is no straight answer. As we discussed earlier, baptism records usually contain less information than civil registration certificates, so it's more difficult to be sure of who is who.

You may have a Thomas Arkwright on your family tree, who married in 1800 in the parish of Ancoats in Lancashire, but there is no proof that the Thomas Arkwright born in that parish 25 years earlier is the same chap. Without a father's name on the marriage record, you have no checking point. What about the Thomas Arkwright who was born in the neighbouring parish in 1802? Or the seven other Thomas Arkwrights who were born in Lancashire parishes within a decade of the one you've found?

Other records sometimes come into play here: you might be able to link family members together using wills, poor law records, monumental inscriptions or other sources. Or you may find that the family you are interested in is the only one of that name in a wide area, or that the name you are researching is so unusual that you feel confident of your facts. But, remember, it's much better to record your uncertainty on your family tree than to spend lots of time and money pursuing the wrong line.

Lots of people find that their research comes to a natural halt when they are unable to distinguish an ancestor from other people of the same name in parish records, at which point they move on to explore other lines or aspects of interest in their tree.

9 What if my ancestor was born in Scotland or Ireland?

There are separate indexes for births registered in Scotland and Ireland, and these are also available online. In the case of Scotland, you can view online copies of actual certificates between 1855 and 1910 at www.scotlandspeople.gov.uk, meaning you can avoid the frustrating wait between ordering and receiving the certificate you want, as you have to do in England, Wales and Ireland.

Later certificates can be ordered through the National Records of Scotland, which includes the General Register Office (GRO) for Scotland. (Note that 'MS' stands for 'Maiden surname' in these records.)

Irish indexes up to 1958 can be searched online at both www.familysearch.org and www.ancestry.co.uk. Offline indexes are available at several repositories, including the GRO's search room in Dublin (from 1864 to the present, excluding Northern Ireland from 1922) and the GRO of Northern Ireland in Belfast. Certificates can be ordered through these organisations.

Indexes and some copies of actual certificates are also available through The Church of Jesus Christ of Latter Day Saints Family History Centres (known as LDS family history centres).

10 I've found birth certificates or baptism records for two children in the same family who appear to have the same name. Can they both be right?

This is quite common and frequently causes confusion to family historians, but usually has a simple explanation. It was common practice among our ancestors to give a child the same name as a deceased sibling.

If they wanted a son called Thomas and the first Thomas died, the next son might also be baptised as Thomas. So, if you come across two children of the same name born to the same parents, look in the death indexes to see if the first child died in between. ■

TAKE IT FURTHER

➡ www.freebmd.org.uk Birth indexes for England and Wales

➡ www.onlineparishclerks.org.uk Place inquiries about records of a particular parish

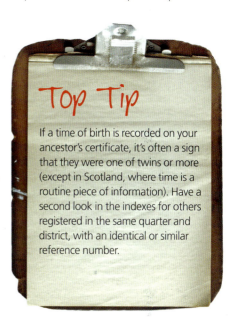

Top Tip

If a time of birth is recorded on your ancestor's certificate, it's often a sign that they were one of twins or more (except in Scotland, where time is a routine piece of information). Have a second look in the indexes for others registered in the same quarter and district, with an identical or similar reference number.

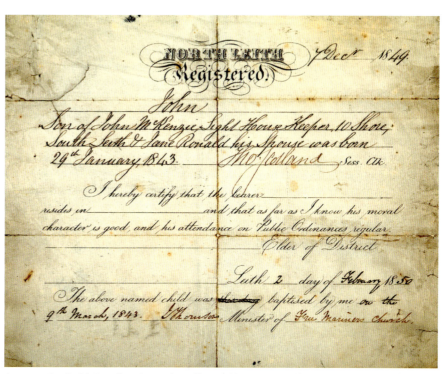

An example of a birth registration and certificate of baptism from Scotland, 1849

Who Do You Think You Are?

A guide to birth certificates

In order to make sure you're extracting the correct information from your family's paperwork, here we dissect Winston Churchill's birth certificate...

1 Date and place of birth

The later the birth certificate, the more likely a full address will appear. A time of birth may mean the baby is a twin, triplet etc.

2 Name

The forename/s given at birth. A line through this column means that no name was given.

3 Father's name

The absence of a name here may mean that the baby is illegitimate. Before 1875, a woman could name any man as the father without having to provide evidence.

4 Name and maiden name of mother

This extra information will help you track down the mother's parents, as well as a marriage between her and the father. From the September quarter of 1911, the mother's maiden name is included in the index.

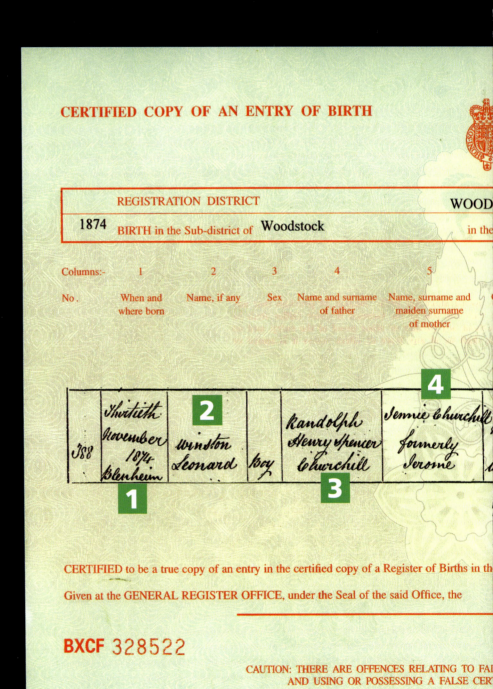

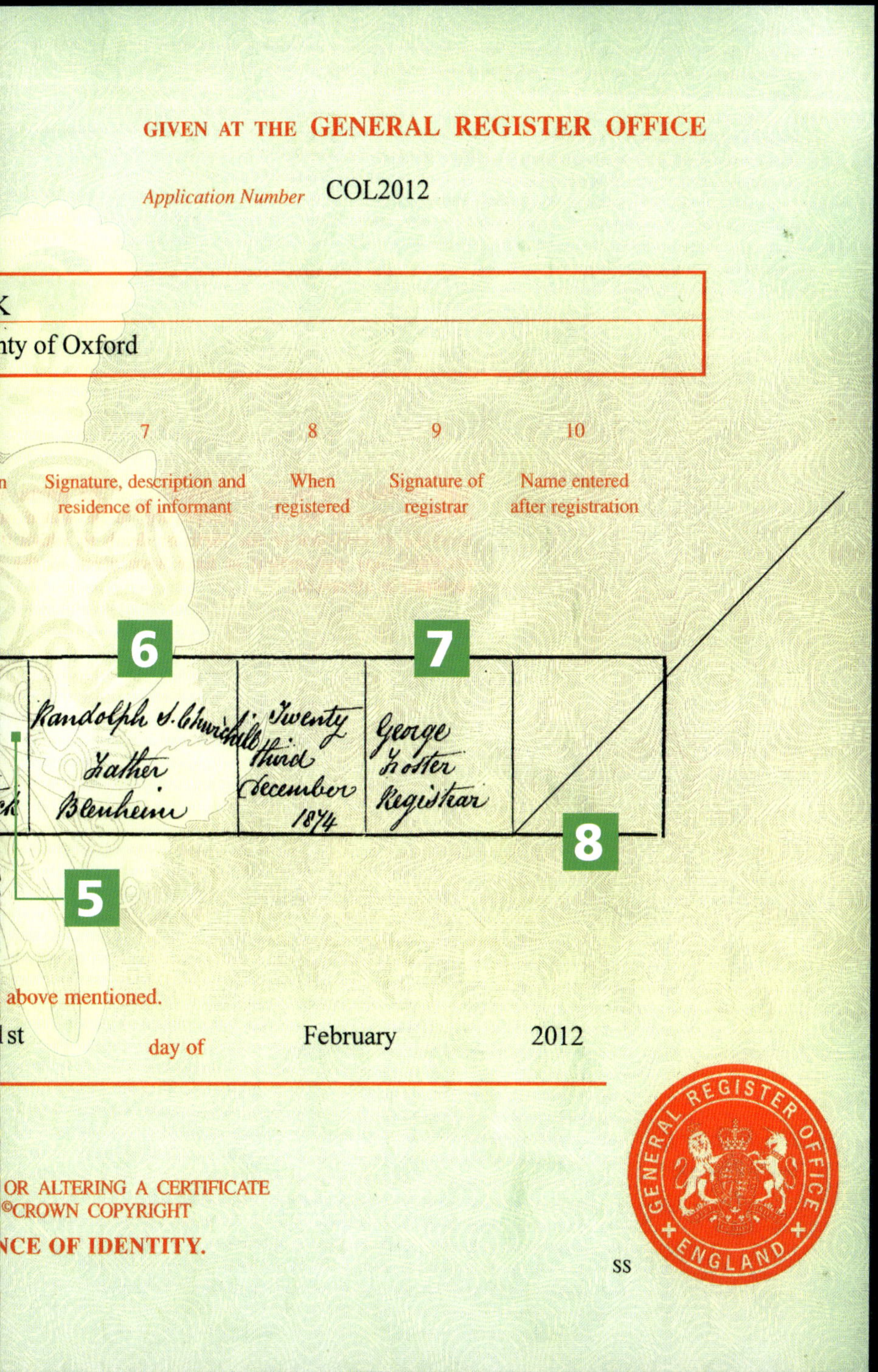

BIRTHS, MARRIAGES & DEATHS
RESEARCHING BIRTHS

GIVEN AT THE GENERAL REGISTER OFFICE

Application Number   COL2012

...nty of Oxford

7	8	9	10
Signature, description and residence of informant	When registered	Signature of registrar	Name entered after registration
Randolph S. Churchill / Father / Blenheim	Twenty third December 1874	George Troster Registrar	

above mentioned.

1st day of February 2012

OR ALTERING A CERTIFICATE
©CROWN COPYRIGHT
NCE OF IDENTITY.

5 Occupation of father

Can be useful for confirming that you are looking at a certificate for the right family – although it is not definitive proof.

6 Signature, description and residence of informant

Usually one of the parents, but it could be a grandparent or other relative. The address is usually the same as the child's place of birth.

7 Date the birth registered

Registration was supposed to take place within 42 days of the birth. This date will determine which quarter the birth appears in the indexes, in this case the December quarter.

8 Names entered after registration

Used to record any names given to the child – for example at baptism – up to 12 months after the initial registration.

Find that marriage!

Marriage records are one of the most important family history sources, says **Jenny Thomas**, who shows you the best methods to pin down that elusive wedding

Marriage records have long been one of my favourite genealogical resources. It is always heart-warming to find a record of an ancestor's marriage. Not only does it represent – and even bring to life for a moment – what we hope was a happy day and the beginning of a fruitful partnership, but the record can be packed with useful information to feed a family tree. And as if these delights were not enough, in terms of finding marriage records, genealogists have never had it so good.

It is now standard to be able to search civil registration marriage indexes by name, rather than trawling through the records quarter-by-quarter and year-by-year. Many websites also carry the facility to cross-check marriage partners – or at least view a list of the other names on the same page of the register.

You are likely to recognise one of these names from your other documents, enabling you to make a positive identification from the indexes of who married whom. Parish records, too, are increasingly easy to access: collections are appearing online so fast that we can barely keep up with them, saving us hours of research time and often considerable travel costs.

However, for those of us not invited to the wedding feast, life can be much more difficult. Some of us come to a frustrating halt as the marriage we want fails to emerge from the records. Surely our great grandparents were married? Their census returns and death certificates say they were; they claim to be married on the birth certificates of their children, so we are

In terms of marriage records, genealogists have never had it so good

understandably annoyed when they fail to appear in the records.

But all may not be lost! We must not give up at the first hurdle. Proof of the marriage may be out there – it might just take a bit more digging. Over the next few pages, I hope to explore some paths that researchers might follow to pin down evidence of an elusive marriage, putting their family history back on the straight and narrow.

Before we begin our quest, we should briefly refresh our minds about some key facts concerning marriage records. Civil registration marriage certificates were produced in England and Wales from 1837, in Scotland from 1855 and in Ireland from 1864 (or 1845 for non-Catholic marriages). You can expect to find substantial information on these certificates, including the date and place of marriage; the names of bride and groom; their ages, occupations, current marital status and residence; the names and occupations of both fathers; the names of witnesses and officiating minister; and the rites under which the ceremony was performed.

In Scotland, the pickings are even richer: the mothers of bride and groom, including maiden names, are routinely recorded on marriage certificates. In the centuries before civil registration, the key resource is likely to be parish records, which in some cases stretch back to the 16th century. These provide invaluable information, but are usually less detailed than civil registration certificates. For example, you are unlikely to find the fathers of bride or groom listed.

Now, without further ado, let's commence our journey down the aisle…

BIRTHS, MARRIAGES & DEATHS
RESEARCHING MARRIAGES

Did your ancestors marry overseas?

It may be that your ancestors married in an unexpected location. The fact that they lived for 50 years in Glasgow, died in Glasgow and had their own children in Glasgow does not necessarily mean that they were married there. The ceremony might have taken place in England, Wales or Ireland, especially if one party originated from or is known to have spent some time there.

Alternatively, your ancestors may have married overseas: perhaps they went abroad as missionaries, civil servants, soldiers, sailors or tourists. They might even have had one or more children abroad: a foreign place of birth for a child on the census might alert you to the possibility that the parents also married overseas. Even if you have no reason to suspect a foreign marriage, the records are worth a peek if you are having no luck elsewhere.

Happily, there are registers of marriages abroad available on many commercial sites: try www.findmypast.co.uk, www.thegenealogist.co.uk, www.familyrelatives.com, www.bmdregisters.co.uk and the 'minor records' on www.scotlandspeople.gov.uk. Certificates can be ordered from the General Register Office in the same way as domestic ones, although they may not always include quite the same level of information.

Remember that there was often no obligation to register overseas events back home, so there is no guarantee of finding a reference even if your hypothesis is correct. Of course, the ceremony is likely to have been recorded in whichever country it took place, but you would need a fairly precise idea of when and where in order to begin a search for these records.

In colonial times, many Brits married abroad, such as this 1899 British wedding in India

Try another index

If you have searched the General Register Office marriage indexes, including all the 'ifs' and 'buts' of name changes and inconsistent spellings, and your ancestors are simply not there, it might be time to check an alternative set of records. Remember that marriages were recorded at the church or wherever the ceremony took place; copies of the registers were then forwarded to be collated by local registrars, after which further copies were sent to be stored and indexed centrally.

It is the central indexes that we search on commercial genealogical websites. But there is always the chance that your ancestors' record slipped through the net at one of the intermediary stages, and you might just strike gold by taking a step closer to the original records. Local indexes are a good place to start; the free website www.ukbmd.org.uk provides links to local indexes that are already online and information about where to access those that are not. Remember that the reference number you obtain from local indexes will not match the General Register Office number, meaning you'll be unable to order a certificate from a local register office using the national reference number, and vice versa.

Parish records

If the record you want still remains elusive, why not go back yet another step and search for the record produced on the day of the ceremony? Many of us have ancestors who married in a church, so parish records might be the next port of call. Parish records can be useful even during the period of civil registration, although you do need to know where

Don't just rely on the central GRO index

your ancestors were likely to have married and have a time frame in mind to search. You may obtain clues from where their children were born or baptised, or the couple might have married in the bride's parish. In Scotland, birth certificates routinely provide the date and place of the parents' marriage – a considerable advantage when seeking the record.

Before the start of civil registration, parish marriage records are likely to be your major source of information. Once again, there are standard search techniques, such as widening your search to include neighbouring parishes, taking advantage of online collections that cover a wide geographical area and being increasingly flexible about spellings the further back you go. Yet, once again, there are other routes you can take if you hit a genealogical brick wall.

Bishops' Transcripts (BTs) were, in theory, copies of parish registers made annually in each parish and sent on to the bishop, but have been known to include more information and entries than the original records. If your ancestor slipped through the parish record net, they may have been caught by the BTs. BTs might also survive where the parish register does not, so it is worth checking if the parish register hasn't survived.

Better late than never

When searching for birth and death records, we are often advised to cover a wider year range than we might have expected, and the same is true for marriage records. There were vast numbers of couples who had their first child nine months or so after the wedding, but this was not always the case!

My favourite example is of a young woman in Scotland who gave birth in the early hours of the morning and appeared at the altar to make her vows later the same day. But a marriage might have taken place months, years or even decades after the birth of the first child, regardless of what it says on the birth certificate about the parents being married. Nobody was likely to know any different at the local register office when the birth of a child and the details of the parents were recorded.

In some localities, it was fairly standard for a couple to marry after the birth of a child; perhaps a husband wanted to assure himself that his wife was fertile before he tied the knot. There was not necessarily any disgrace attached to this. Attitudes varied widely and these might become part of your research into your ancestors' times. In many instances, a child was legitimised by the subsequent marriage of the parents, leaving them free of the difficulties that might disadvantage a legal bastard.

Conversely, a couple might have married and produced no children for ten or more years, leaving researchers baffled as to why there is no marriage record a year or two before the arrival of offspring. It is therefore important to widen your search to cover all eventualities. It is much easier now, in the days of name-indexed marriage records, to search large numbers of years in one go, but many of us still instinctively restrict our search to encompass only the narrow spectrum in which we expect the record to appear.

Not all marriages will be found nine or more months before the first child is born

Were they married at all?

Family photos may give clues to help track down a marriage

You should also consider the possibility that your ancestors were not officially married at all, even if they claimed and were assumed to be so all their lives.

Many are the times that I've come across a couple living as husband and wife, registering their children as a married couple, but for whom there is no evidence whatsoever of a formal union. It may be that they simply considered themselves to be married, whether in the eyes of God or the law, or intended to marry one day but never quite got round to it. The law and how it was interpreted could be complicated in this respect, while there was sometimes conflict between church law and civil law.

What we might now call common law marriage was certainly practised by some of our ancestors, although this was supposedly ended by Hardwicke's Marriage Act of 1753, which applied to England and Wales and decreed (among other things) that all couples except Jews and Quakers must marry in an Anglican church for the union to be valid. Similarly, in Scotland, simply declaring oneself to be married was sometimes deemed sufficient. Such informal arrangements were unlikely to have produced any paperwork.

However, if a couple failed to marry, it is worth asking yourself why this might have been. Would they easily have resisted the joy of a wedding ceremony, of being centre-stage for a day and formalising their union, unless there was a reason? As actor Robert Lindsay discovered, the reason may be that one party was married already! See also Martin Freeman's case study opposite.

Remember that the genealogical details you were hoping to find on your ancestors' marriage certificate may be revealed through other sources, particularly the census – and perhaps even the certificate of a previous or subsequent marriage.

BIRTHS, MARRIAGES & DEATHS
RESEARCHING MARRIAGES

Were they nonconformist?

During the period of civil registration, a marriage certificate should have been produced in the same way, regardless of the religion of the couple or the rites and ceremonies under which the union took place. The same is not true in earlier centuries. The majority of our ancestors would have married in the established church – usually the local parish church – but others were nonconformist and chose to marry elsewhere. Perhaps they were Catholics, Quakers, or Baptists and married in their own denominational church or chapel.

They will, therefore, be recorded in a separate set of records, many of which are available online at www.bmdregisters.co.uk, www.familysearch.org, www.scotlandspeople.gov.uk and www.ancestry.co.uk. Different denominations were tolerated to different degrees during the turbulent centuries of our history: we have already discussed Hardwicke's Act, and its insistence that all marriages be performed in an Anglican church.

This did not stop all nonconformist marriages from taking place, but substantially reduced the numbers. In many cases, there would have been a risk attached to keeping clear records of marriages that were performed illegally, so even if a ceremony took place, paperwork may not have been produced or have survived.

Of course, your ancestors might not have been of a Christian denomination at all. They might have been Jewish and legally entitled to marry under those rites. A record of the ceremony might appear in the records of the relevant synagogue or as part of a larger amalgamated collection.

A Quaker wedding taking place in 1881

CASE STUDY FROM THE SHOW
MARTIN FREEMAN

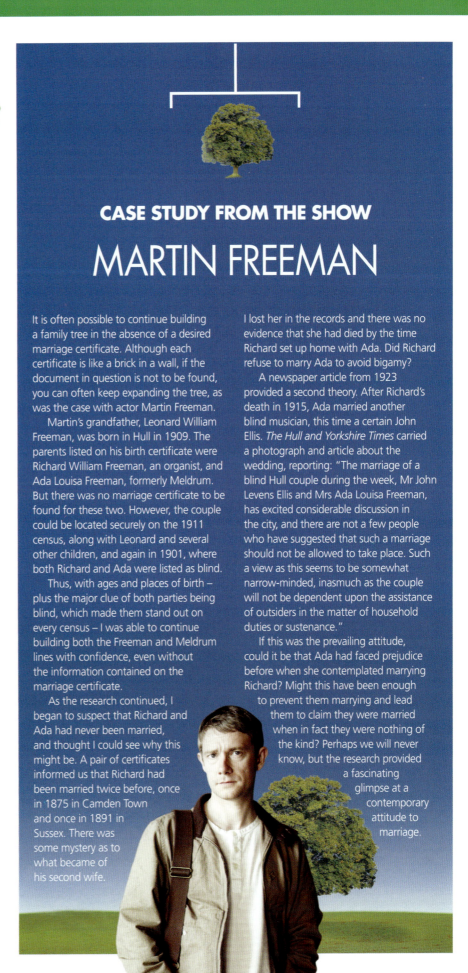

It is often possible to continue building a family tree in the absence of a desired marriage certificate. Although each certificate is like a brick in a wall, if the document in question is not to be found, you can often keep expanding the tree, as was the case with actor Martin Freeman.

Martin's grandfather, Leonard William Freeman, was born in Hull in 1909. The parents listed on his birth certificate were Richard William Freeman, an organist, and Ada Louisa Freeman, formerly Meldrum. But there was no marriage certificate to be found for these two. However, the couple could be located securely on the 1911 census, along with Leonard and several other children, and again in 1901, where both Richard and Ada were listed as blind.

Thus, with ages and places of birth – plus the major clue of both parties being blind, which made them stand out on every census – I was able to continue building both the Freeman and Meldrum lines with confidence, even without the information contained on the marriage certificate.

As the research continued, I began to suspect that Richard and Ada had never been married, and thought I could see why this might be. A pair of certificates informed us that Richard had been married twice before, once in 1875 in Camden Town and once in 1891 in Sussex. There was some mystery as to what became of his second wife.

I lost her in the records and there was no evidence that she had died by the time Richard set up home with Ada. Did Richard refuse to marry Ada to avoid bigamy?

A newspaper article from 1923 provided a second theory. After Richard's death in 1915, Ada married another blind musician, this time a certain John Ellis. *The Hull and Yorkshire Times* carried a photograph and article about the wedding, reporting: "The marriage of a blind Hull couple during the week, Mr John Levens Ellis and Mrs Ada Louisa Freeman, has excited considerable discussion in the city, and there are not a few people who have suggested that such a marriage should not be allowed to take place. Such a view as this seems to be somewhat narrow-minded, inasmuch as the couple will not be dependent upon the assistance of outsiders in the matter of household duties or sustenance."

If this was the prevailing attitude, could it be that Ada had faced prejudice before when she contemplated marrying Richard? Might this have been enough to prevent them marrying and lead them to claim they were married when in fact they were nothing of the kind? Perhaps we will never know, but the research provided a fascinating glimpse at a contemporary attitude to marriage.

Always check for photos and invitations in your family's possession

Try other marriage records

Although genealogists are correct to seek the official documentation that was produced at the time of their ancestors' marriage, there are various other documents that might indicate, and in some cases prove, that the marriage in question took place.

There might be a report of the marriage in a local newspaper, perhaps even including a photograph of the happy couple on the big day. It is a tremendous advantage when searching newspapers to know when and where the ceremony took place, but as more and more local newspapers become available online, the scope for speculative searching increases.

The British Library's digitisation project is adding pages all the time to its British Newspaper Archive (britishnewspaperarchive.co.uk), while the National Library of Wales is currently digitising its newspaper collection. You might also find notice of a couple's engagement in a local or national newspaper (did your ancestors announce their engagement in *The Times*? Have a look at The Times Digital Archive at http://archive.timesonline.co.uk/tol/archive to find out), but remember that the announcement of an engagement does not necessarily mean the marriage took place.

Have a look for photographs preserved in your family collection of the bride and groom on their wedding day, or letters, invitations or other documents that make reference to the event. There may also be information to replace or supplement a civil registration marriage certificate at the relevant place of worship. For example, Nigella Lawson was lucky enough to find a contract for her ancestors' marriage at the West London Synagogue. The ceremony took place in 1863 and the contract laid out the terms

In parish records, it is worth looking for banns or a licence

and conditions of the union, detailing the amount of money that the bride would receive in case of a divorce – a greater sum if she was a virgin!

In less happy circumstances, divorce files are available at The National Archives, indexed on their website and on www.findmypast.co.uk 1858-1903. The files often carry a copy of the marriage certificate and information about why the marriage failed.

When searching in parish records, it is worth looking for a record of banns or a marriage licence, as well as the record of the actual marriage. Hardwicke's Act formalised centuries-old customs, meaning couples wishing to marry were obliged to have banns read in their respective parish churches for three Sundays before the ceremony in order to give anyone who wanted to issue a challenge a chance to do so. Alternatively, the couple could apply for a marriage licence from a bishop, archbishop or archdeacon. This would avoid the three-week delay, especially handy if there was danger of a child arriving before the wedding took place. It could also be something of a status symbol, not least because a fee was required for a licence.

In order to obtain a licence, it was customary for the groom to swear that there was no impediment to the marriage – the 'allegation' – and often a sum of money was laid down which would be forfeit if an impediment was found. This was the 'bond'. These documents can contain valuable genealogical information.

Banns book

The fact that banns had been read should have been recorded along with the parish record or in a separate 'banns book'. It is worth investigating whether a separate book survives for your ancestors' parish if the marriage register does not. If so, it is likely to be held in the relevant local record office. The same is true of marriage licences, allegations and bonds, although licences issued by archbishops are more likely to be held in the collections at Lambeth Palace for Canterbury or the Borthwick Institute for York.

Collections are also making their way online, for example at www.ancestry.co.uk and www.familysearch.org. If you do find evidence of marriage banns or a licence, it is well worth re-examining the original parish records for the period immediately afterwards. After all, you know exactly when the ceremony should have taken place and it may well be that the record slipped the index, but is correctly contained in the original registers.

BIRTHS, MARRIAGES & DEATHS
RESEARCHING MARRIAGES

Irregular and clandestine marriages

One of the central aims of Hardwicke's Act was to clamp down on 'irregular and clandestine marriages', thousands of which took place annually. Couples who did not have parental consent, who wished to marry away from their home parish or for whom there was some impediment might choose this route. The Fleet Prison was a favourite place for such unions. It did not fall under church jurisdiction and its clergymen could usually be persuaded to turn a blind eye to standard procedure in return for a fee. Such marriages became a profitable industry: it's estimated that, before 1753, as many as half of marriages that took place in London were conducted in or near the Fleet Prison.

The first records of Fleet Marriages date from the early 17th century, and many of the records we refer to as 'Fleet Registers' are available online at www.bmdregisters.co.uk and www.familysearch.org. The National Archives' podcast on the subject of Fleet Registers is also well worth a listen.

It is unwise to assume that everyone who married at The Fleet was in some way dishonest or disreputable, although there were certainly bigamists, people seeking false documentation and all kinds of reprobates among them. Plenty of perfectly regular marriages were conducted at The Fleet. A couple might simply have wished to avoid the expense of a wedding in their own parish, or their hands might have been forced by opposition to the match among their families.

To Gretna Green…

As soon as the Hardwicke's Act was in place, people started to find ways round it. Its great flaw was that it did not apply to Scotland, so couples wishing to avoid the terms of the Act simply went north of the border and tied the knot. The most popular destination for such unions was the famous Gretna Green. A collection of marriages held in the village is available on www.ancestry.co.uk. ■

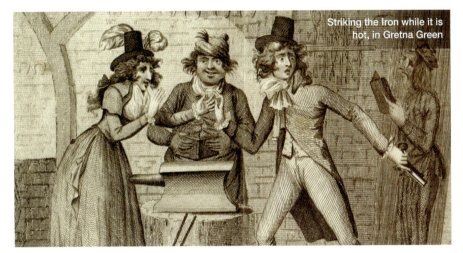
Striking the Iron while it is hot, in Gretna Green

TAKE IT FURTHER

➡ **www.britishnewspaperarchive.co.uk**
Search newspaper wedding announcements

➡ **www.ukbmd.org.uk** A free-to-use website for searching births, marriages and deaths

---

Step-by-step guide to finding a Fleet marriage

STEP 1:
Enter the relevant name on bmdregisters.co.uk
You can search the indexes of nonconformist and 'other' marriages for free, but if you want to narrow down results using the advanced search function, you need to register and buy credits.

STEP 2:
Choose from the possible matches
If you haven't used the advanced search, then you can spot Fleet marriages because they belong to record set RG7. Viewing the original or a transcription will cost 5 credits each (£5 for 10 credits).

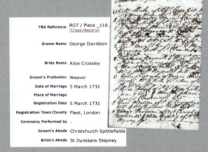

STEP 3:
View a transcription and the original
Because 18th-century handwriting can be difficult to read, you may want to look at both the transcription and the original. Remember pay-per-view can add up, so it could be worth looking at a Gold or Diamond subscription to TheGenealogist.co.uk which include credit-free access to these records.

How to date old family wedding photos

Rebecca Arnold guides you through the early 20th-century wedding fashions that will help you date those unidentified family snaps

▶ Around 1912-1915

Style
Styles had begun to change around 1907 when brides began to wear plainer dresses like the one in this photograph.

Groom
The groom wears a smart morning coat and striped trousers. He also has a top hat.

Hemline
Tabard-like layers were very popular. The bride's skirt just reaches the top of her shoes – the hemline would slowly edge up in subsequent years.

Dress
Previously popular tight corsetry is abandoned. This bride's dress focuses on her narrow waistline.

Bodice
Her bodice has blouse-like reveres and a small, raised collar – these became fashionable around 1912.

▶ Around 1914-1916

Veil
The veil is extravagantly long. Note that the bride's hair is almost covered and the veil sits low on her head.

Dress
Many wartime brides wore simple suits, but this one has a silk dress and a full, wide bouquet.

Hemline
Her hemline is slightly raised and her dress has some fullness at hip level.

Groom
The groom wears army uniform, but there are no identifying badges or indications of rank. This may be because he had only just been called up, or perhaps he was a Conscientious Objector about to go to France to work as a medic.

Train
Wartime brides often had to improvise due to fabric shortages and rationing. However, in this case, the bride wears an elaborate gown, with all the accessories associated with a fashionable wedding.

BIRTHS, MARRIAGES & DEATHS
RESEARCHING MARRIAGES

▶ Around 1920-1924

Bouquet
The bride's bouquet is full, with a variety of flowers and a few trailing fronds.

Veil
Her veil is fairly long and wide, and is gathered into a neat headdress that covers most of her hair – a similar style was worn by Lady Elizabeth Bowes Lyon in 1923 when she married the future King George VI.

Dress
Her ankles are visible and the hemline of her dress (and that of her little bridesmaid) is scalloped – a popular decoration at the time.

Group
This wedding group typifies the outdoor photographs of the 1920s. Simple styles are enlivened by subtle decoration and interesting headwear.

Groom
The groom wears morning dress and spats on his shoes – as does the best man.

▶ Mid-late 1930s

Style
This wedding combines high fashion references with Hollywood-inspired glamour. This was the decade when wedding dresses began to develop their own styles – often drawing upon historical references.

Evening Wear
By this time, evening – rather than day – dress was the main influence. This bride's gown epitomises the idea of a special dress to be worn only once.

Groom
The groom wears morning dress – a black coat and waistcoat with grey trousers.

Dress
Her dress has a long train, swathed to the front for the photograph, and an equally voluminous veil. Although the dress uses a lot of fabric, the overall style is simple – with emphasis on drapery at the hem and across the bodice.

Who Do You Think You Are? 45

A guide to marriage certificates

Wedding certificates hold crucial details to unlock mysteries in your family tree. Here is the paperwork from Arthur Conan Doyle's second marriage...

1 Married in...

Normally the parish church, but you may find a nonconformist chapel recorded here, along with indication of whether your ancestors were married by licence.

2 When married

This marriage happened on 18 September, 1907, so it will be found in the indexes for the September quarter.

3 Name and surname

The names given by the bride and groom at the time the marriage took place.

4 Age

The age given by the bride and groom is only as accurate as they believed it to be. If it says 'Of full age', it just means the bride or groom was over 21.

5 Signatures

The certificate you receive from the GRO is a copy of the register. It doesn't show actual signatures, but will show if your ancestors could sign their name. Those who couldn't marked an 'x'.

BIRTHS, MARRIAGES & DEATHS
RESEARCHING MARRIAGES

6 Witnesses

Always check the witnesses on a marriage certificate as they may reveal family connections and add to your tree.

7 Condition

This shows the marital state of the parties. 'Bachelor' or 'spinster' for those who had not married before; or 'widower/widow' or 'marriage dissolved'.

8 Rank or profession

Don't assume a woman did nothing to earn money if there is no entry next to her name. It is common to find only the groom's occupation.

9 Residence

The address given here can be misleading, as some couples used a temporary address to qualify for marriage in the parish. Some just name the parish.

10 Father's name and profession

These details are vital for checking you have the right certificate. No recorded name would suggest illegitimacy.

A death can create more records than a life

Records of death

Jenny Thomas shows how using death records can reveal a multitude of new genealogical details to fill in the blanks on your family tree

When genealogists first build their family trees, the temptation is to only gather birth and marriage certificates, using them like rungs in a ladder to climb quickly from one generation to the next. This is all very well, but there's a danger of neglecting an essential resource: death records. It's possible that more records were created when your ancestor died than at any time during their life. And these can be packed with information about their circumstances, family, property, friends and other personal details.

It's also difficult to properly understand an ancestor's life without knowing anything about the timing and circumstances of their death. For instance, it makes a great deal of difference to how you might interpret your great grandmother's life if you know that she outlived her husband by 50 years, if she lived to see all her daughters married or, if after years of hardship, she ended her days in the workhouse and was buried in a pauper's grave. And knowing that your great grandfather died in 1920 as opposed to 1910 makes a vast difference: it might mean he lived long enough to see his sons killed in the war or receive military honours; he may have witnessed world events that he would otherwise never have dreamed about; it could mean that he received the vote before he died. Death records really are the third corner of a genealogical triangle, and happily more are becoming available online all the time.

Death certificates

During the period of civil registration (from 1837 in England and Wales, 1855 in Scotland and 1864 in Ireland), death certificates are often your first port of call when investigating the end of an ancestor's life. These documents provide details that should enable you to be confident you've correctly identified your ancestor, and often to supplement your existing knowledge of them. Full name; age; date, place and cause of death; occupation (for women, this is often "wife of" or "widow of", and for children "son of" or "daughter of"); and the identity of the informant are among the details included. So you may discover that your ancestor died away from home, suffered from an illness prevalent in their time or met a particularly interesting end.

In some cases, the length of time of the last illness is recorded, so you might see "diabetes – 2 years" or "paralysis – 3 months", which

BIRTHS, MARRIAGES & DEATHS
RESEARCHING DEATHS

Bringing home the dead from Llanerch colliery explosion, 1890

may help paint a picture of the last days, weeks or years of their lives. Scottish death certificates go one step further: they additionally record the names of the parents of the deceased, which can shoot your family tree back an extra generation.

Death certificates can turn up all kinds of surprises that help complete or adjust your ideas about an ancestor. Actress Dervla Kirwan, for example, found that her luckless great grandfather Henry Kahn died in a lunatic asylum in 1907, a telling consequence of the hardship, prejudice, ill-health and injustice he had suffered during his life. And it was a death certificate that alerted Griff Rhys Jones to the fact that his great grandfather Daniel Price had not been killed in a train crash, as the family thought, but was killed by a certain John Thomas. The death certificate recorded manslaughter and indicated that an inquest had been held. The reports of this inquest – and the relevant court records – enabled Griff to continue his investigation.

Indexes to death certificates are available online and, in the case of Scotland, many of the actual certificates are online. For England, Wales and Ireland, copies of certificates can be ordered from the relevant General Register Office (GRO).

Burial records
Whether or not you are working in the period of civil registration, a burial record can be a useful asset. First and foremost, ▷

Step-by-step guide to ordering a death certificate

When you have identified reference details for your ancestor in the death indexes, you'll need to order a copy of the actual certificate to see the information it contains. If there are several options of the same name, similar age and similar location, you may need to order more than one certificate or consult other sources to be sure you've found the right one.

STEP 1:
Knowing that Daniel Price died in Llanelli between the 1891 and 1901 censuses, we searched FreeBMD. Commercial websites carry more complete death indexes.

STEP 2:
Note the details of the result – in this case, found in the June quarter of 1897: you will need this information to order a copy of the actual certificate.

STEP 3:
Go to the website of the GRO for England and Wales. You need to register, enter the certificate details and pay for it online. The cost is currently £9.25 for each certificate.

Who Do You Think You Are? 49

▷ during the pre-civil registration era, a parish burial record will tell you roughly when your ancestor died. The range of information provided on a burial record varies widely: the name of the deceased and the date and parish of burial are standard. Beyond this, you may be lucky enough to find an age, residence, occupation, family member, cause of death or other details. I have even seen comments such as "dead of the plague" or "a reputed witch" alongside burial records. Whatever the period, knowing where your ancestor was laid to rest can provide a meaningful location for a family pilgrimage.

There are impressive collections of burial records online. It was in the online National Burial Index that Kevin Whately discovered the resting place of two ancestors at St John the Baptist church in New Malden, Surrey. A visit to the tomb revealed further details that prompted a new line of research.

If you are unable to find records online, you may have to investigate offline parish records at family history centres or at local or county record offices. For more recent burials, I sometimes strike gold simply by contacting the burial grounds closest to where the ancestor died.

Obituaries

Whether or not your ancestor was a noteworthy figure in their day, they may have warranted an obituary in the local newspaper. Obituaries can provide all kinds of interesting details about the departed: their life, career and achievements; their interests; the offices they held; the names of mourners at the funeral and a hundred and one other details. You may uncover information that doesn't appear in other sources or that points you in the direction of further resources. For example, Richard Madeley learned from an obituary in a Canadian newspaper that his great great grandfather, John Murdoch, was a retired farmer, a staunch Methodist and a political friend of the prime minister of Canada. And Robin Gibb's midwife ancestor, Cecilia Lynch, was described in her heart-warming 1939 obituary as "one of the most popular figures in the district", indicating that her reputation had recovered following a previous prosecution.

Once again, increasing numbers of newspapers are available online, while offline collections are held at local records offices and at the British Newspaper Library at Colindale in North London. It's a good idea to search in every available local paper for two or three weeks after the death, as occasionally different obituaries appear in different publications, supplementing one another's information.

If your ancestor lived in one place but died in another, you might be advised to search in both locations. Remember, too, that if the deceased belonged to a particular group or trade, its specialist publication or magazine might contain a relevant death notice or obituary. Emilia Fox, for example, found her thespian great great aunt Lily's death reported in *The Stage* in 1908. You may have to hunt a little to find these specialised publications, but if the organisation or industry has its own archive, that's the best place to start.

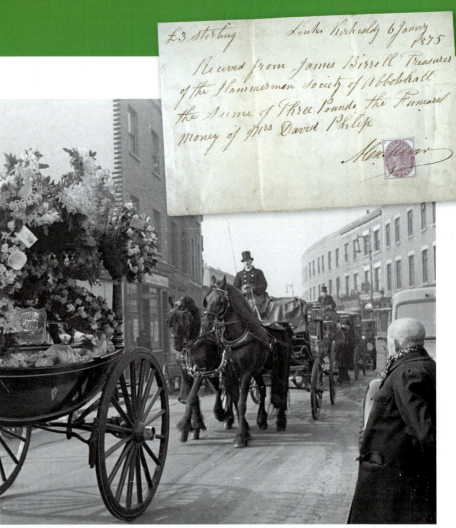

Records relating to your forebears funeral can shed light on their life, as well as potentially offer clues to the next step on your journey of discovery

Check burial records as well as death certificates

> "Your ancestor may have warranted an obituary in the local newspaper"

BIRTHS, MARRIAGES & DEATHS
RESEARCHING DEATHS

Inquests
Although the official inquest report into an ancestor's death may have been destroyed or is still deemed confidential (check this with the relevant local record office), proceedings are likely to have been reported in some detail in the local newspaper. Griff Rhys Jones turned to a Llanelli newspaper to find out more about Daniel Price's untimely death and discovered that, although some witnesses claimed that John Thomas brutally set upon Daniel as he walked home from the pub, another crowd of witnesses from the pub agreed that it was more of a mutual fight with an equal level of aggression from both quarters.

Trouble at sea
If your ancestor died in a larger-scale incident, you may find that although newspaper reports don't focus particularly on your ancestor, you can still find plenty of details about the circumstances in which they died. If you're fortunate enough, you may even find a mention of them by name. When Monty Don's great great grandfather, the Reverend Charles Hodge, was drowned in a shipwreck off Anglesey in 1859, the catastrophe was eagerly reported in both the local and national press, including mention of Charles himself. *The Liverpool Mercury* reported how Charles had encouraged the victims to pray during their last moments, while references were made in *The Manchester Weekly Times* to the reverend's troubled domestic circumstances.

It may be that following a disaster such as a maritime, mining, railway or industrial accident, there was an official inquiry that may, again, have been reported in the newspapers. Other records may survive in The National Archives or local record offices. ▷

CASE STUDY FROM THE SHOW
RICK STEIN

Indexes of deaths registered abroad proved to be an invaluable asset when researching chef Rick Stein's family tree. Rick's grandmother, Mary Henrietta Parkes, had been born in Canton, China, in 1877, the daughter of Henry Parkes, a missionary.

Keen to find out more about the family's time in China, we searched the birth and death indexes for British citizens abroad and found two references for deaths of Parkes children. They turned out to be Ellen Eliza Parkes, aged six, who died in July 1873 and John Henry Parkes, aged one, who died less than a month later, both the children of Henry Parkes. These certificates did not contain a cause of death, so Rick would have to turn to other sources to find out more.

He searched in letters sent by Henry to the missionary authorities in England, begging to be allowed to come home for the sake of his family's health. He reveals that he is very anxious about the prospect of spending another summer in China following the deaths of two of his children.

Rick discovered that epidemics periodically ravished Canton – cholera, smallpox, typhoid and even plague. No wonder Henry was afraid!

However, there were no more deaths in the registers for the Parkes family and Rick was grateful to know that his grandmother and the other Parkes siblings survived into adulthood in good health.

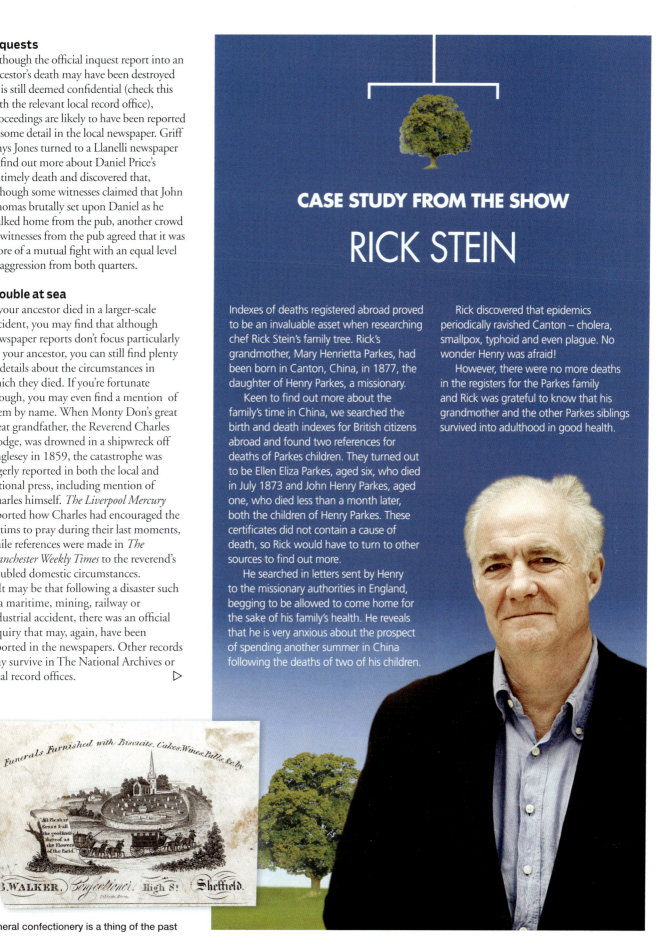

Funeral confectionery is a thing of the past

Deaths overseas

Occasionally no matter how hard we look, we cannot find the required death certificate in any UK index. It may be that a forebear died abroad, and it is always worth checking the relevant records. There are separate lists of UK nationals who died overseas, or indeed at sea, and many of these records are available at sites such as **www.findmypast.co.uk** and **www.thegenealogist.co.uk**. These lists will not be comprehensive, but they are a good start to your investigation. Certificates of UK nationals who died overseas and appear in these indexes can be ordered from the General Register Office in the same way as domestic ones.

Certificates of ancestors who died overseas may contain less information than domestic paperwork. When *WDYTYA?* researchers investigated Rick Stein's missionary ancestors in China, they located two relevant entries in the indexes of deaths overseas. But although the certificates revealed that two young children of the family had died in the 1870s, no cause of death was recorded. It was letters sent from their father in China to the missionary authorities in England that filled in this gap by discussing an outbreak of cholera, plague and other illnesses in the area.

One of the most common circumstances for deaths overseas is when people were serving in the military. Although you might

There are records available for those who were buried at sea

find your ancestor's reference in the online indexes of armed forces deaths, you are likely to find scant detail on the actual certificate. However, other records may serve you better. If you are tracing a death in either of the two World Wars, the Commonwealth War Graves Commission (**www.cwgc.org**) is an excellent resource. Search for your ancestor by a range of information, and discover details such as rank, service number, date of death, age, regiment or service, next of kin and burial details. Remember to check their local newspaper for an obituary.

You may also be able to find death or burial records in the relevant foreign country, depending on what has survived, along with obituaries and monumental inscriptions. The wills of British citizens who resided temporarily or permanently abroad might be found in UK collections, especially if they owned land or property here.

Records of those who died in British India are available in The British Library India Office, which has impressive collections available online through its website at **http://indiafamily.bl.uk/UI/Home.aspx**. Records are also available through the Families in British India Society's website, **www.fibis.org** and **www.findmypast.co.uk** from February 2014.

▷ Monumental inscriptions

If you're fortunate enough to find a monumental inscription for your ancestor, you may discover not only dates of birth and death, and who was related to whom in your family, but also some personal characteristics of the ancestor in question, particularly the affection in which they were held.

Jeremy Irons learned from a monumental inscription to his great great grandfather, Henry Loftie Rutton, who died in Ireland, not only that Henry had been born in Ashford, Kent, but that two of his children had died young and were buried with him: one aged 17 and one aged 23. David Mitchell found an inscription in Kilmore churchyard to his clergyman ancestor John Forbes: the gravestone says that John died on 21 January 1867, aged 52, and that the stone had been erected by his congregation as a mark of their esteem for him.

Once again, there are growing numbers of monumental inscriptions available online; a few minutes spent on a search engine often produces some results. It is, of course, helpful to know when and particularly where your ancestor was buried, before you begin your search.

Many genealogists find themselves having to undertake journeys to visit the graveyard in question to hunt down the memorial to their ancestor, but remember that local and national record offices and family or local history societies may have been there before you, transcribed the inscriptions and deposited them in their archives. This is especially helpful if the churchyard in question no longer exists, or if the inscriptions have become so worn that they are becoming illegible. The genuki website www.genuki.org.uk can be a useful tool for tracking these records down.

Remember that if your ancestor was involved in a particular organisation, there might be a plaque or monumental inscription in a relevant place: for example, inside their church for a clergyman, inside their professional headquarters, or on the wall of a club or society to which they belonged.

Wills and probate records

Wills can be a magnificent source of information about a departed ancestor, as they can tell you about the goods and chattels that they left behind – often including very personal bequests, such as books, jewellery or the tools of their trade. You might learn about who was in or out of favour by the legacies awarded; you might learn something of your ancestor's attitude to their family, friends and the world in general; the location of the property they owned; what kind of a funeral they wanted; to whom their daughters had

BIRTHS, MARRIAGES & DEATHS
RESEARCHING DEATHS

married; which of their children were still minors; who their friends, executors, servants or business partners were; and a host of other details that you would be hard pushed to find elsewhere.

A will can also serve to sum up an ancestor's position and achievements during the course of their life. Nigella Lawson realised just how far her great great grandfather Barnet Salmon had come in the world by examining his will: born into poverty, he left £46,000 when he died in 1897. This translated to almost £3.5 million in today's terms – a testimony to his business acumen. In less cheerful circumstances, the will of David Mitchell's ancestor, John Forbes, exposes rifts within his family: not only does John proclaim that he will leave nothing to his intemperate wife, but that his daughters are to inherit only on the condition that they make good marriages – and even then, the money is for the use of the daughters alone, rather than their husbands. The document certainly belies any notions David had formed of John Forbes's domestic bliss.

Getting hold of a will can sometimes prove something of a challenge. After 1858, the system was centralised in England and Wales, and copies of wills after this can be obtained through the Principal Registry of the Family Division in London. Before 1858, however, the documents are scattered according to the ecclesiastical court in which they were proved, which in practice means that many are held in the collections of the Prerogative Court of Canterbury collection (online), the Prerogative Court of York collection (at the Borthwick Institute) or in local records offices.

However, your task of tracking down the document you want is rendered considerably easier by the many collections of actual wills, or indexes to them, that are available online – not least the National Probate Calendar, on www.ancestry.co.uk, which may point you in the right direction. A research guide is available on the National Archives website at www.nationalarchives.gov.uk/records/research-guides/wills-and-probate-records.htm. Welsh wills can be searched for free at www.llgc.org.uk.

In Scotland, an even greater proportion of wills are online: the ScotlandsPeople site, www.scotlandspeople.gov.uk, hosts wills and testaments 1500-1900, and later material is available in various archives. These resources include The National Records of Scotland (www.nas.gov.uk). In Ireland, the system was once again centralised in 1858, with responsibility for proving wills passed from ecclesiastical courts to the Principal Registry. However, much material from both before and after 1858 was destroyed in the famous 1922 fire, although various indexes and copies survive.

The National Archives of Ireland (www.nationalarchives.ie) and the Public Record Office of Northern Ireland (www.proni.gov.uk) are good places to begin your search. When you are searching for an ancestor's will, remember to have a look for other related sets of records that might embellish the information it contains.

Death duty registers – which are indexed online for England and Wales – may tell you something about the value of an estate and what happened to it in practice (whether or not this complied with the terms of the will), while inventories may provide a fascinating and usually very detailed glimpse into the contents and furnishings of your ancestor's property. ∎

> "A will can sum up an ancestor's achievements during the course of their life"

You may be lucky enough to uncover mourning or 'In Memoriam' cards

The funeral of a member of a well-to-do family, c1733

TAKE IT FURTHER

➡ **www.deceasedonline.com** Burial and cremation records from mid-19th century onwards

➡ **www.origins.net** Contains the invaluable and expanding National Wills index – and more

Who Do You Think You Are?

A guide to death certificates

Death certificates don't just record the cause of death. They can also hint at the life of the deceased. This is Florence Nightingale's certificate...

1 Where and when died

This column should provide date and a location or full address. The relative may have died at work, putting it in a different registration district than the one you're expecting.

2 Name and surname

The name given to the registrar by the informant. This will be the name they were using at time of death, not always their birth name.

3 Age

The informant gives the deceased's age at death to the best of their knowledge, so tread carefully: it won't necessarily be correct.

4 Occupation

The last known occupation of the deceased. Females were usually described by their relationship to their husband or father – for instance, 'widow of'.

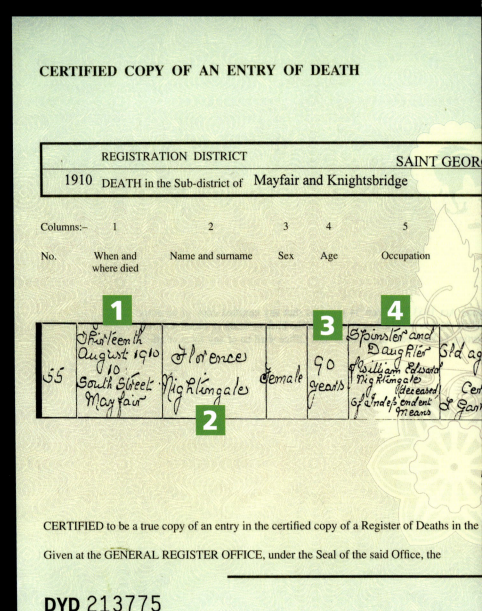

BIRTHS, MARRIAGES & DEATHS
RESEARCHING DEATHS

5 Cause of death

If the word 'certified' appears, it means the cause of death was given by the doctor in medical attendance of the deceased. If there was an inquest, that will also be noted.

6 Signature, description and residence of informant

Often a spouse or other close relative. If the address is the same as the place of death, then it's likely the deceased died at home. After 1875, the relationship to the deceased was declared.

7 When registered

The date that the death was registered. This was usually very shortly after the death, as a certificate was needed before a burial could take place.

The census was, and still is, a snapshot of what lies behind the nation's front doors

HOW TO:
Use the census to find your ancestors

Censuses can reveal a great amount of detail about how your ancestors lived their lives. **Jenny Thomas** shares her insider knowledge on how best to use the paperwork to make your family tree grow

The release of the 1911 census in 2009 sent the world of genealogy buzzing. In the intervening years, fascinating stories have emerged about the people who appear in the census and what it tells us about their lives. Thousands of researchers have been able to make progress with their family trees, revelling in a fresh set of data or demolishing brick walls that had previously stood in their way.

Those unfamiliar with the census as a research tool might have felt rather bemused by all the excitement surrounding 1911's release. What is the significance of the census? What, indeed, is a census? Why do genealogists rave about it, and how can a beginner gain access and use it to build their family tree? It's time to go back to basics, and examine the cake upon which the 1911 census is the current icing.

The census was, and still is, a snapshot of the population of the country. Its aim was to list every person, household by household, street by street, according to where they spent

CENSUS 1841–1911

a single, specified night known as 'census night' – whether they were at home with their family, visiting friends, at boarding school, in hospital, in prison, on a boat or anywhere else. And it was not only names that were listed: age, marital status, relationship to the head of the household, occupation, place of birth and, of course, where they spent the census night are the staples of genealogical research.

This kind of information really feeds a family tree. If you find your great grandfather as a child on the census, you may discover for the first time that ten brothers and sisters were also squeezed into the same household.

If you've always wondered why your grandmother never talked about her father, you may find that he doesn't appear on census returns, but that his wife was a widowed head of household. You may think your great uncle came from Manchester, but the census will explain he was actually born in Ireland.

Nuts and bolts

The census was taken every ten years, beginning in 1801. The motives were many and varied, but a desire to know how many people of military age, or otherwise, there were in the country – as well as an increasing interest in issues of health and overcrowding – must be counted among them. The census returns for 1801, 1811, 1821 and 1831 are not very useful because they did not record the majority of names – they served primarily as head counts. It is the returns from 1841, 1851, 1861, 1871, 1881, 1891, 1901 and 1911 that dominate family history research. They are all available and indexed online.

The country was divided into registration districts and sub-divided into enumeration districts – the area one 'enumerator' or census taker could cover in a day. The enumerator would deliver 'schedules' (blank census forms) to each household in their patch and it was the responsibility of the head of household to see that it was filled in – whether by a member of the household, a literate acquaintance or the enumerator themself. The enumerator would then collect the schedules, sort and copy them, before sending them off to London. With the exception of 1911, the actual schedules filled in by the householders do not survive.

Understandably, the information found on census returns is not always completely accurate. There were many stages at which corruptions could creep in. Not only were names, ages and spellings less important than today, but, for example, if a housewife believed (or wished) that she was 38 rather than 46, that would be the age recorded on the schedule. If her son William George was known as George in the family, then he will probably be referred to as George in the census. The information given wasn't checked.

In addition, if a third party completed the schedule, they would record what they heard – or thought they heard – and probably make a stab at spelling unfamiliar names and places. If the enumerator or subsequent copyists could not read the writing, they too would have made a guess, as would those who eventually transcribed the online indexes. By understanding how the census was compiled, we are equipped to search for our ancestors with a flexible approach.

> *Its aim was to list where every person, street by street, spent a single, specified night – 'census night'*

Watch out!

Don't assume that anyone of the right name on the census is bound to be your ancestor. You'll need to back up your finds by checking that other known family members are present and correct, cross-referencing with certificates and other sources.

The details of all household members were recorded, family and staff alike

Who Do You Think You Are? 57

Watch out!

Don't be distracted by crossings out on your census returns and discount potentially crucial details. These were made as data was counted and do not mean that the information is wrong.

> # The census is the closest thing we have to stepping into our ancestors' homes

▷ At the simplest level, the census can be used to trace your ancestors at ten-yearly intervals. For instance, if your grandfather was 25 in 1911, you might find him as a 15-year-old in the household of his parents in 1901 and as a little boy of five in 1891. You might then search for his parents in their pre-marriage households, discovering the names of their parents, and so on back through the years.

Unless your ancestors had very unusual names, you will need to use the census in conjunction with the other pillar of family tree building – birth, marriage and death certificates – in order to confirm who is who and to acquire precise names, dates and addresses. But from the census, you may learn about siblings and other relatives, be alerted to missing members of a household (perhaps children who died between one census and the next), note changes of circumstance and catch a glimpse at where and in what context your ancestors were living. The census is the closest thing we have to stepping across the threshold of their home. ∎

What the different years tell us

1841 (Taken on 6 June)
The information requested consisted of: address (usually vague, for example, just the name of a street or village); name; age, which was rounded down to the nearest five years for those over 15; sex; occupation; whether born in the county in which they are currently residing, or in Scotland, Ireland or foreign parts.

1851 (Taken on 30 March)
Address; name; relation to head of family (for example, head, wife, daughter, nephew, visitor, lodger, inmate); marital status (married, unmarried, widow); age; sex; rank, profession or occupation; where born; whether blind or deaf-and-dumb.

1861 (Taken on 7 April)
Exactly the same information as 1851 was requested of householders.

1871 (Taken on 2 April)
The same as 1851, with the exception of the last column, which asks whether the individual is deaf-and-dumb, blind, an imbecile or idiot, or a lunatic.

1881 (Taken on 3 April)
The same as 1871.

1891 (Taken on 5 April)
In addition to the information recorded in 1881, householders were asked to declare how many rooms in the house were occupied, as well as whether individuals were an employer, employed or neither. In the Welsh census, an extra question was added about language spoken, to which the standard replies were Welsh, English or both.

1901 (Taken on 31 March)
As well as the information on 1891 returns, householders were also asked whether they worked at home.

1911 (Taken on 2 April)
Added to the information requested in 1901, women were asked to declare the number of complete years their current marriage had lasted, the number of children born alive within this marriage, the number still living and how many had died.

People were also asked to state the industry in which they worked, the number of rooms occupied and the age at which deafness, blindness or other infirmity began. Whoever filled in the schedule will have signed it, so you can tell to which of your ancestors the handwriting belongs.

Watch out!

There are some standard abbreviations that regularly appear on census returns: for example, "Ditto", also often written as "Do" or "do". Names are often shortened; George William might appear as Geo Wm and Elizabeth Mary might be Eliz M or simply Eliz.

Scottish & Irish census

Scottish and Irish censuses were taken in much the same way as their English and Welsh counterparts, and people were asked substantially the same questions. But there are important additions and differences to note, the most distressing of which is that virtually no Irish census returns survive for the years before 1901.

Scotland

Scottish census returns from 1841 to 1911 are available online at www.scotlandspeople.gov.uk. Censuses are customarily confidential for 100 years to protect the privacy of those who appear in them, but the 1911 census for England and Wales was released in 2009, two years before the due date. Scotland, however, operates under different Freedom of Information rules and so the 1911 census wasn't released for public access until April 2011, after the standard century of closure.

There might be differences in the release of information, but when it comes to that information's collation, the questions asked in the Scottish census are substantially the same as in England and Wales. In 1841, people were asked to state whether they were born in the county in which they were living, or born in England, Ireland or foreign parts (rather than Scotland, Ireland or foreign parts, as in the English census). In 1891 and 1901, they were also asked whether they spoke Gaelic, English or both, although this column is often blank in the returns. In 1861 and 1871, people were asked about the number of rooms in their dwelling that had one or more windows, and how many children aged between five and 13 were attending school or, in 1871, being educated at home. In 1881, 1891 and 1901, the question about the number of rooms with one or more windows was repeated.

Ireland

Most (but not quite all) material from the earlier Irish censuses has been destroyed, some accidentally by fire, while others were pulped during the First World War. Some were deliberately destroyed shortly after they were taken, possibly to preserve privacy once the necessary statistics had been extracted. However, the 1901 and 1911 censuses survive almost in their entirety and are now available to view online on the National Archives of Ireland site (www.census.nationalarchives.ie).

The 1901 Irish census recorded address; name; relationship to head of household; religion; whether each person could read and write; age; occupation; marital status, place of birth and whether English or Irish was spoken. Questions were also asked about the house itself: the materials from which the house and the roof were built, the number of rooms and windows, whether there were outhouses, and the overall class of the property. Researchers can build a clear picture of the domestic situation and relative wealth or poverty of their ancestors, as well as spot any change for better or worse.

The 1911 census additionally asked married women to declare the number of years of the current marriage, the number of children born alive within the marriage and the number of these children still living.

Scottish householders were asked to record how many windows each of their rooms had

Who Do You Think You Are?

An 1881 census return

Here we investigate how to read a Victorian census return, one completed by an apparently wealthy family – and their domestic staff – in their home on Upper Belgrave Street in Knightsbridge

1 Location of census

This information will help pinpoint your ancestor's general location.

2 Relation to head of family

As well as head, wife, son or daughter, here you might also find servant, visitor, in-laws, border, lodger, companion, inmate or pupil.

3 Marital status

Often M or Mar for married; S, U, Un, Unm for single/unmarried; W, Wid or Widr for widowed.

4 Age

The age an individual believed to be correct, or would admit to. Generally given in years, although a small m indicates age in months.

5 Double vertical lines

These handwritten enumerators' marks are the symbol signifying the start of a new household.

6 Street name and number

The address gives a good indication of the quality of housing in which your ancestor lived. Check its location on local maps of the time.

CENSUS
1841–1911

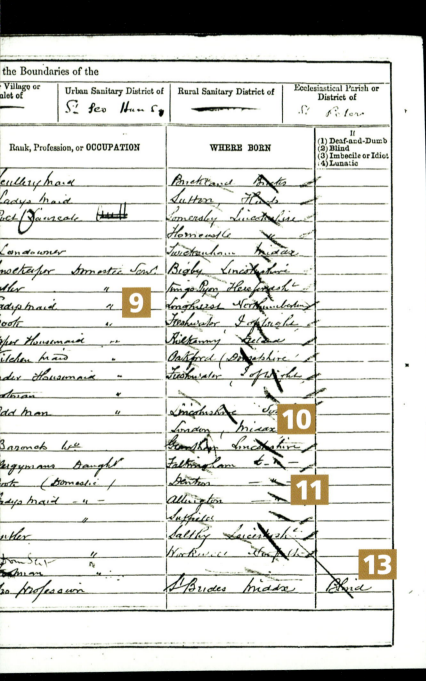

7 Name
Nobody in this household is recorded with a middle name or initial, but this does not mean they don't have one.

8 Gender
This is denoted along with the age, where the information is recorded in different columns for males and females.

9 Rank or occupation
In such a prestigious household, everyone here is listed according to their precise job. But job descriptions may be exaggerated.

10 Where born
Enumerators may have misheard or misspelt place names and your ancestor may have written different things on each return.

11 Crossings out
Crossings out do not mean the entry is wrong; it is a later mark made when statistics were gathered.

12 Reference number (RG 11) and piece number (98
The former denotes the census year (here 1881) and the latter can be an indication of location.

13 Infirmity
Here, it will indicate if your ancestor was blind, deaf and dumb, imbecile or lunatic.

Who Do You Think You Are?   61

A 1911 census return

The Beckham family of Walworth in 1911 (the ancestors of David Beckham) comprised three generations, in either employment or education, and living in modest conditions

1 Quality of copies

The original householders' schedules have been removed from their old files, conserved and scanned in colour. The original documents are in very good condition considering their age.

2 Generations

Three generations of the Beckham family lived in one household. William, his wife and children, plus his parents John and Sarah.

3 Particulars as to marriage

William and his wife Harriet had been married for 30 years, having had ten children. Sadly two had since died. Seven were still living with their parents; presumably an older child had left home.

4 Occupations

Note the occupations of John, a scavenger (a dustman or refuse collector), and his son William, a carman (a driver of a cart). William, the head of the household who presumably completed the schedule, noted their industry as "Bow Council" so we know who both men worked for. The clerks' occupation codes of those in employment are noted, in this case, in green ink. These classification numbers are explained at 1911census.co.uk.

5 Living conditions

This three-generation household of 11 people lived in confined accommodation – just six rooms, excluding bathroom or sculleries.

6 Infirmities

Details whether residents were "totally deaf", "deaf and dumb", "totally blind", "lunatic", "imbecile" or "feeble-minded".

7 Signature

This is the original householder's schedule, which has all the information and more than is noted in the transcription. William Beckham signed the schedule and it looks like he completed it too.

CENSUS 1841–1911

HOW TO:
Find a missing ancestor

During the research for *Who Do You Think You Are?*, we frequently have trouble locating an ancestor on the census. Sometimes this provides an enjoyable challenge: it is tremendously satisfying to undertake some detective work and catch an elusive ancestor in our genealogical net. But there are occasions, too, when no amount of searching comes up with the goods. We almost imagine that we can hear an ancestor sniggering at us from across the years, from their hiding place among the records.

On occasion, we never find the missing census return, although the family is present and correct on every other census. Common sense dictates that in a complete set they should be there to be found. Certainly there are times when someone is simply not on the census. Not only have small portions of various censuses not survived, but individuals and families might have not been counted, whether deliberately or accidentally. Some people would have been abroad for their work on the night a census was taken, perhaps as mariners, soldiers or commercial travellers. The wealthy might have been taking pleasure trips abroad. Others may have emigrated, either temporarily or permanently, and may appear on foreign records.

A less-than-assiduous enumerator could have missed one or more households. And there is no doubt that some people were so suspicious of the recording of their data, or perhaps afraid of revealing exactly who and what they were, that they avoided being counted. There are tales of suspicious Londoners rowing out into the Thames on census night to avoid being recorded – and of equally determined enumerators rowing out after them. Not everyone was happy about declaring personal information; they didn't necessarily understand the purposes for which it was collected, nor how it was going to be used. The same issues are hotly debated today.

There is also no doubt that some of our ancestors would have lied – or been mistaken – about their personal details, so that they are unrecognisable to the genealogist attempting to research them. Individuals and families often changed their names, ages, occupations and places of birth – sometimes beyond recognition – between one census and the next.

If a family member was not present on the night of the census, they wouldn't have been recorded

However, it is sometimes tempting for a frustrated genealogist to abandon their investigation and to accept that an ancestor is not to be found, when in fact he or she is present and correct – when some deeper digging will unearth them. Around three-quarters of the returns that present an initial challenge are uncovered in the end.

How the census was collected

In order to understand the problems involved with searching a census, it is important to recognise how the online indexes available to genealogists came to be. The information collected by the census enumerators was provided by (often illiterate) householders, who could not check the spellings or other details that went down on their returns. If the enumerator did not know how to spell a name or place, he would probably simply have guessed and hoped for the best.

Neither was there any check on the information provided, and if someone gave a false name or incorrect details, they were likely to get away with it. The returns were then collected and copied, and the indexes made much later from the copies. Clearly, there were several points at which errors could creep in, or individuals could accidentally slip from the records.

In addition, those who have done the invaluable job of compiling census indexes were not in a position to know what a family name 'should' be. When researching the Zurhurst family for Sheila Hancock, we discovered that the indexer had listed the family under 'Tarhorst' – which was indeed how the name appeared on the return. ■

Genealogy researcher Jenny Thomas worked on seven series of Who Do You Think You Are?

▶▶ **Turn the page for hints on how to find an ancestor 'hidden' in a census**

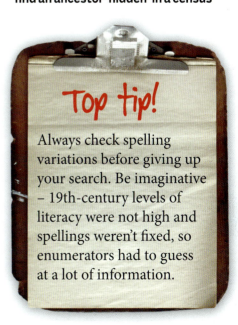

Top tip!

Always check spelling variations before giving up your search. Be imaginative – 19th-century levels of literacy were not high and spellings weren't fixed, so enumerators had to guess at a lot of information.

Who Do You Think You Are?

Six easy tips for finding an ancestor who is hidden in the census

1. Change the parameters of your search

If your initial search produces no results, try Soundex searches (these look for names that sound like the one you're looking for, available on some sites), wider age ranges and less exact places of birth. The more precise information that you enter into the search box, the more chance there is of your ancestor being excluded from the results because something doesn't quite match. People may be listed under a middle name; the Gunn family may appear as Gun or Dunn; William may be Wm; a woman might be listed as 55 although you calculate that she is 62; and an ancestor may claim to have been born in West Derby on one census and Liverpool on the next. For instance, an elusive ancestor, whose initials (not his name) were entered on the return could be located simply by entering his age and place of birth. Perhaps dispense with surnames altogether and use the other search criteria to narrow down the options, or succeed in finding a set of siblings by entering a surname alone and an age or place of birth.

2. Search for other people you would expect to find in the same household

If one ancestor does not spring to light, try looking for their siblings, wife or children, or search the location in which you would expect to find them. Conversely, remember that families were not always together on census night: members might be at work, at sea, in service, in prison or visiting friends, so extend your search to every family member and likely location and you may get lucky.

House numbers often changed, so extend your search to include neighbouring residences

3. Run address searches

You might have an address for your 'hidden' ancestor from other documents and, if they appear to be missing from a census, look at the document nearest in date and search under that particular address. It is a good idea to extend the search for a few census pages either side of the expected address, as house numbers sometimes changed, and families often moved to properties very nearby.

4. Employ the services of another pair of eyes

Many are the times that one genealogist simply cannot find an ancestor, but another researcher picks them up almost straight away. It is always worth asking someone else to check the records.

Visit our forum at http://forum.bbcwhodoyouthinkyouare.com for assistance or advice from others. Also see if anyone is researching the same family. You could even employ a professional genealogist.

5. Try a different website

If you are having no luck with one index, try a different website that has an independent index. It may be that your ancestor is correctly indexed in one when they are hidden in another. Also, depending on your browser or type of PC, you may encounter problems with some websites. The various census search sites use a range of different criteria or options to perform the searches, so depending on the type and amount of information you already have, some websites may be able to search more efficiently. If you are worried about the expense of using other websites, first check that they definitely employ different indexes to search, then use them on a pay-per-view only basis.

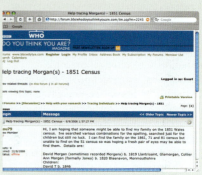

If a search is not bearing fruit, try another website with a differently compiled index

6. Generate more information by researching either side of the problem census

If you are still stuck with a certain census, it is often useful to find the ancestor on the censuses before and after, and then return to the one that is causing problems. Other returns will confirm names, ages and locations, and may provide evidence of other family members or alert you to variations in personal details that may help in the search. And finding an ancestor on a later census is, of course, a very good way of proving that they were still alive during the period you're searching, even if they are tricky to track down.

When all else fails…

There may come a point, however, when you admit defeat and accept that you are not going to find the census return that you want. However, all is not lost. There are other records that can provide information to substitute for a missing census return:

Use birth, marriage and death certificates

Use birth, marriage and death certificates to establish names and addresses for a family, as well as ages and occupations. Often evidence of a family's movements and employment over a period of 10 or 20 years is provided through the birth certificates of their children. You can establish the kind of area in which they were living and, with the help of maps and local histories, make an informed guess as to what the accommodation would have been like – and whether there was likely to have been sufficient room for guests, lodgers or servants, the type of information found on censuses.

Check street and trade directories

Local street and trade directories are a good way of locating at least the head of household in the years when you can find no census return – and, indeed, in the years between one census and the next. Equipped with an address from a previous census or other documents, annual street directories may help you to establish how long a family lived at a certain address. If your ancestor was listed in the trades section and was conducting their business from home, you should also be able to trace any change of abode. You may also find other people living or conducting business from the same premises.

Local and tax records

Local land and tax records or tithe maps may help to pinpoint ancestors, especially the valuation survey of the 1840s. In Ireland, *Griffith's Valuation* is a substitute for absent census material.

Other material

Occupational records, newspaper articles, obituaries, family letters, wills, diaries, deeds and other material that you uncover as you continue your research may provide addresses – or, at least, clues as to the area in which your ancestor lived at a particular time. They may also mention occupations, servants, live-in relatives or companions – again, revealing information found on the census.

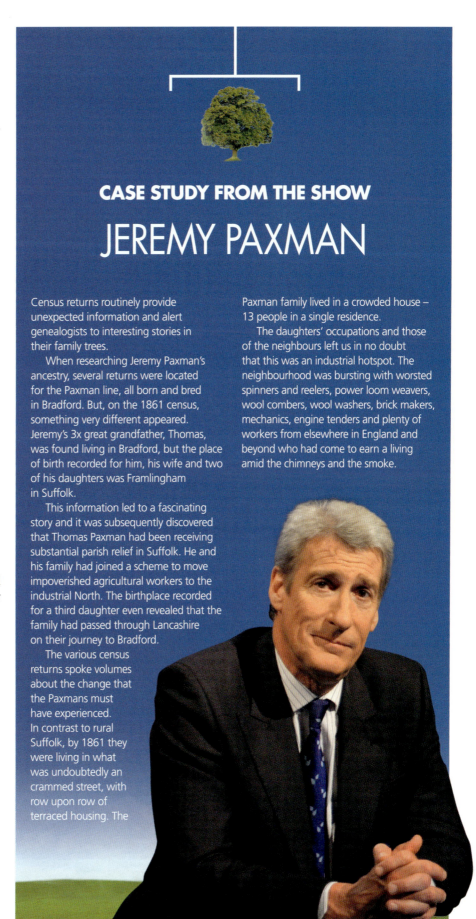

CASE STUDY FROM THE SHOW
JEREMY PAXMAN

Census returns routinely provide unexpected information and alert genealogists to interesting stories in their family trees.

When researching Jeremy Paxman's ancestry, several returns were located for the Paxman line, all born and bred in Bradford. But, on the 1861 census, something very different appeared. Jeremy's 3x great grandfather, Thomas, was found living in Bradford, but the place of birth recorded for him, his wife and two of his daughters was Framlingham in Suffolk.

This information led to a fascinating story and it was subsequently discovered that Thomas Paxman had been receiving substantial parish relief in Suffolk. He and his family had joined a scheme to move impoverished agricultural workers to the industrial North. The birthplace recorded for a third daughter even revealed that the family had passed through Lancashire on their journey to Bradford.

The various census returns spoke volumes about the change that the Paxmans must have experienced. In contrast to rural Suffolk, by 1861 they were living in what was undoubtedly an crammed street, with row upon row of terraced housing. The Paxman family lived in a crowded house – 13 people in a single residence.

The daughters' occupations and those of the neighbours left us in no doubt that this was an industrial hotspot. The neighbourhood was bursting with worsted spinners and reelers, power loom weavers, wool combers, wool washers, brick makers, mechanics, engine tenders and plenty of workers from elsewhere in England and beyond who had come to earn a living amid the chimneys and the smoke.

Take your research further online...

From our newsletter to Facebook and Twitter, there are lots of ways to discover new leads online

NEWSLETTER

Delivered straight to your inbox every week, our free newsletter is packed with the latest family history stories and details of online data releases, plus TV listings with the shows you'll love. Simply visit the link below and register.

- ✓ The latest online records
- ✓ Great offers & competitions
- ✓ Weekly TV and radio guide
- ✓ Blogs from the magazine team

www.whodoyouthinkyouaremagazine.com/newsletter

TWITTER

Keep in touch with the team and get the latest genealogy news as it happens with the magazine's Twitter feed.

twitter.com/wdytyamagazine

NEW

FORUM APP

Our new app lets you make the most of our community of family historians from your smartphone or tablet. Search for **WDYTYA Forum** via the App Store or Google Play.

FACEBOOK

Find out about new record releases and what we're up to in the office – plus win some great prizes every week!

www.facebook.com/whodoyouthinkyouaremagazine

whodoyouthinkyouaremagazine.com

OUT AND ABOUT
50 HIDDEN GEMS

50 Hidden gems around the UK

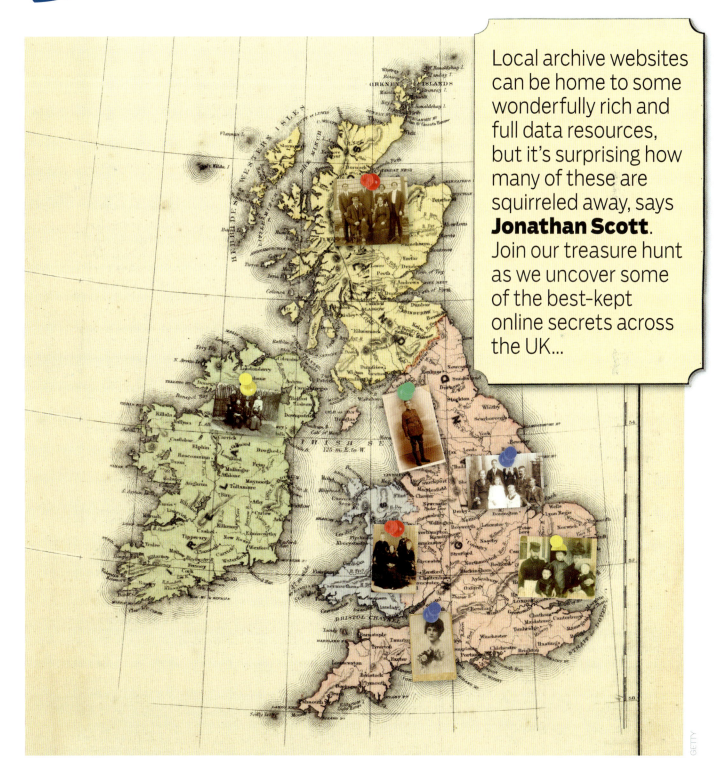

Local archive websites can be home to some wonderfully rich and full data resources, but it's surprising how many of these are squirreled away, says **Jonathan Scott**. Join our treasure hunt as we uncover some of the best-kept online secrets across the UK…

Who Do You Think You Are?

SOUTH-EAST

1 Berkshire Record Office
Berkshire probate collection
Price: £25
🖥 www.berkshirerecordoffice.org.uk
The index to the Archdeaconry of Berkshire probate collection (1480-1857) provides names, dates, residences and occupations of over 39,000 people. The CD is available either at Berkshire Record Office or online via the Berkshire Family History Society. There are also online exhibitions on Victorian Broadmoor and Fair Mile Hospital.

2 Centre for Buckinghamshire Studies
Wills database
Price: £5 per will
🖥 www.buckscc.gov.uk/bcc/archives/online_resources.page?
Between 1483 and 1858, the Archdeaconry of Buckingham Court proved over 35,000 wills of Buckinghamshire people. You can search the index and then order copies online. There's a similar service for parish register collections (copies or searches are £5 each), plus free databases of Victorian prisoners in Aylesbury Gaol and trade directories.

3 Essex Record Office
Essex Ancestors
Price: Ranges from £5 for 24hrs to £75 for an annual subscription
🖥 http://seax.essexcc.gov.uk
Essex's catalogue, Seax, remains free to use, and searches will often lead to free digital images of records. Meanwhile, images of Essex parish registers – including various London boroughs – and wills are now available via new subscription site Essex Ancestors.

4 Hampshire Archives and Local Studies
Hampshire wills
Price: Free
🖥 www3.hants.gov.uk/archives/catalog.htm
Hampshire's online catalogue allows users to search through an index of over 110,000 wills by name. You can print out and complete a form to order copies for a fee. In addition, there are 15,000 digital images including 10,000 photographs.

5 Hertfordshire Archives and Local Studies
Hertfordshire Names Online
Price: Free
🖥 www.hertsdirect.org/services/leisculture/heritage1/hals/indexes/
Hertfordshire Names Online gives you access to Hertfordshire Archives material and Local Studies indexes to all sorts of local and family history sources, such as pre-1837 marriages, wills, newspapers, court registers, archive catalogue index and records about the poor.

6 Bedfordshire and Luton Archives
Gaols and pubs
Price: Free
🖥 www.bedfordshire.gov.uk/archive
The site includes Bedfordshire Pubs, which draws on records of buildings, breweries, publicans and patrons to give detailed histories. There's also a free Bedfordshire Gaol register database (1801-1879).

7 Kent History Online
Births, Marriages and Deaths
Price: Free
🖥 www.kent.gov.uk/leisure_and_culture/kent_history/kent_history_online.aspx
Search births, deaths and marriages in Kent since 1 July 1837, then apply for a certificate by phone/post. There are links to Kent probate material available via Origins, an online catalogue (currently being bolstered by images of some of the records) and a free database of 88,000 pages of council records.

8 Kingston-upon-Thames
Burial registers
Price: Free
🖥 www2.kingston.gov.uk/GraveRecords
This smart and easy-to-use website is a searchable database of burials at Kingston and Surbiton cemeteries, which allows you to view an image of the original burial register for free, recording the day and even the hour of burial.

9 London Metropolitan Archives
The Family History Research Service
Price: Varies
🖥 www.cityoflondon.gov.uk/things-to-do/visiting-the-city/archives-and-city-history/london-metropolitan-archives/family-history/Pages/default.aspx
The Family History Research Service is designed for people who are unable to visit the archives in person. Their enquiry team can tell you about the records they hold and, for a fee, can also conduct research on your behalf.

10 Medway Archives and Local Studies Centre
Medway parish registers
Price: Free
🖥 www.medway.gov.uk/leisureandculture/libraries/archivesandlocalstudies.aspx
Medway Ancestors gives you free access to images of original parish registers from the Archdeaconry of Rochester, covering the Medway parishes and extending into areas of north-west Kent, such as Dartford and Gravesend. There's also a free index of local newspapers going back to 1830.

11 Portsmouth City Council
A Tale of One City
Price: Free
🖥 www.ATaleOfOneCity.portsmouth.gov.uk
This new community website needs to attract more users to really establish itself, but could be a goldmine as it invites visitors to add pictures, memories and stories to build an online archive of Portsmouth's history.

12 Southampton Archives Service
Merchant seamen
Price: £15
🖥 www.southampton.gov.uk/s-leisure/artsheritage/history/maritimehistory
Although you can't search online, this page gives you information about Southampton's maritime sources, including crew lists and a Central Index Register of Merchant Seamen – with over 1.25 million service record cards. You can request a search in the latter for £15.

13 Suffolk Record Office
Suffolk Heritage Direct
Price: Free
🖥 www.suffolkheritagedirect.org.uk
Explore a huge range of material through Suffolk's excellent online

A 1950s sporting event from the Centre for Buckinghamshire Studies photographic collection

OUT AND ABOUT
50 HIDDEN GEMS

catalogue, which draws on databases from Suffolk Record Office, Britten Pears Library, plus several museums. It includes images of objects, artefacts, photographs and documents.

14 City of Westminster Archives Centre
Settlement Examination Index
Price: Free
www.westminster.gov.uk/services/libraries/archives/indexes
Scroll down to the 'Indexes and Finding Aids' to use the name index to the parish of St Martin-in-the-Fields settlement examination books (1732-1775). There's also an index to Westminster streets covered by the Survey of London, an ongoing architectural history published by English Heritage.

SOUTH-WEST

15 Bath Record Office
Bath Ancestors database
Price: Free
www.batharchives.co.uk
Trace your Bath-residing forebears via this online database which covers the years 1603-1990 and takes its information from original records held by the Record Office. At present, just over half of the indexes (transcribed by volunteers) are available online, with more following. The original documents may well contain more information; copies of them can be ordered for a small charge.

16 Bristol Museums, Galleries and Archives
'Know Your Place' project
Price: Free
www.bristol.gov.uk/page/know-your-place
Explore this fully interactive map charting Bristol's heritage, with linked historic maps, images, information about famous landmarks and buildings, and oral history recordings. The enhanced version requires the free Silverlight plug-in.

17 Gloucestershire Archives
Genealogical database
Price: Varies
www.gloucestershire.gov.uk/archives/article/107400/Genealogical-database
This database contains an index of names drawn from wills proved at Gloucester (1541-1858), inventories, nonconformist baptisms for some chapels, records of the Overseers of the Poor, and gaol registers (1815-1879). You can order copies of some of the archive's records via its website.

18 Somerset Record Office
Oral history clips
Price: Free
www.somerset.gov.uk/archives
Browse and listen to audio clips (along with transcripts) from the Exmoor and Somerset Voices oral history archive. There are also indexes to Somerset Wills (1812-1857), Bridgwater Shipping Crew Lists (35,000 entries) and prisoners in Ilchester Gaol (1821-1844).

MIDLANDS

20 Derbyshire Record Office
Probate database
Price: Copies from 25 pence
www.derbyshire.gov.uk/leisure/record_office/records/wills/default.asp
The record office, which is undergoing refurbishment, has a database of wills from between 1858 and 1928. The wills cannot be viewed online, but you can order copies for a small fee.

There's also a free database of prisoners in the County Gaol and houses of correction (1729-1913).

21 Lincolnshire Archives
Lincs To The Past
Price: Free
www.lincstothepast.com
Launched in May 2011, you can search over half a million resources from the county's collections, including images of parish registers, and specific collections, such as the database of nearly 2,000 convicts transported from Lincolnshire between 1788 and 1868.

22 Warwickshire County Record Office
Victuallers database
Price: Free
www.warwickshire.gov.uk/countyrecordoffice
County sources are available via Ancestry.co.uk, catalogues via ▷

19 Wiltshire and Swindon History Centre
Wiltshire Wills project
Price: £5
www.wshc.eu/wiltshire-wills-project.html
Wills and inventories can give valuable information about people's financial status and property, family relationships and friendships. Wiltshire Archives houses the Salisbury Diocesan Probate collection – 105,000 wills dating from 1540 to 1858. The records of the diocese of Salisbury used to cover not only Wiltshire but also Berkshire and parts of Dorset and Devon. As part of the Lottery-funded Wiltshire Wills Project, staff are taking digital images of every item and making them available to view online. From this page you can read background information about the various types of probate records, before clicking through to the search page.

You can search the catalogue for free by filling in the fields in the left-hand menu bar, by name, place, occupation and date. To view the records you will need to register with the e-shop first. In search results, a scanner icon indicates that an online image is available.

There's a standard charge of £5 per entry for an online image, which you can then print or copy to your hard drive. If an image is not yet available, you can still order print-outs or photocopies – and the minimum charge is £5.

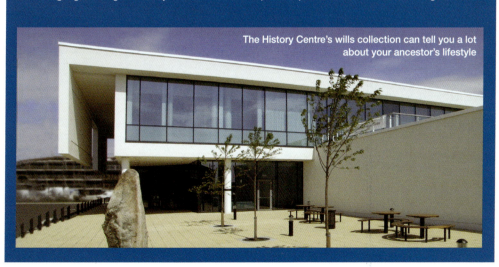
The History Centre's wills collection can tell you a lot about your ancestor's lifestyle

22 Staffordshire and Stoke-On-Trent Archive Service
Staffs Name Indexes
Price: Free to search, ordering prices vary
www.staffsnameindexes.org.uk

An apprenticeship indenture for an agricultural engineer, 1896

You can quickly and easily search through a number of key Staffordshire databases here, namely: the Calendars of Prisoners at Staffordshire Quarter Sessions (1779-1880); Staffordshire Police Force Registers Index (1842-1920); Diocese of Lichfield Wills (1650-1730); Staffordshire Apprentices (1600-1900); Workhouse Admissions and Discharges (1836-1900); Tenants of the Manor of Newcastle-under-Lyme (1700-1832); Parish Clerks, Diocese of Lichfield (1691-1916); Stafford Gaol Photograph Albums Index (1877-1916); and finally, Quarter Sessions Jurors Lists Index (1811-1831).

It's possible to order copies of many of these records. To take the Calendars of Prisoners as an example, each transcript costs £7. There's also an excellent and fully indexed website based around the Sutherland Papers collection (www.sutherlandcollection.org.uk), an archive created by the Leveson-Gower family, Marquesses of Stafford and Dukes of Sutherland, which contains many thousands of names and free access to some document images/transcripts.

Warwickshire's Past Unlocked web page (http://archivesunlocked.warwickshire.gov.uk/CalmView) and images via the excellent Windows on Warwickshire site (www.windowsonwarwickshire.org.uk). There's also a victuallers' database containing details of licensed victuallers in Warwickshire (from 1801-1828), an index to Calendars of Prisoners (1800-1900) and a tithe apportionments database.

24 Wolverhampton Archives and Local Studies
Burial indexes
Price: Free
www.wolverhamptonhistory.org.uk/resources/familyhistory
This excellent resource allows you to track down a host of burial records from across the county. The information available includes indexes to many local parish and Merridale Cemetery registers, monumental inscriptions and Wolverhampton wills. These can all be found by clicking on the 'Indexes' button on the left-hand side of this page. Each individual index is available as a PDF document, which you can then download to your computer.

25 Worcestershire Record Office
Tithe and inclosure maps
Price: Free
www.worcestershire.gov.uk/cms/archaeology/information-and-advice/tithe-and-inclosure-map-project.aspx
Alongside free indexes (including absent voters, apprentices, watchmakers, and births, marriages and deaths information, which has been extracted from Berrows Worcester Journal), you'll find the Worcestershire Tithe and Inclosure Map Project. This provides access to digitised 18th- and 19th-century maps, with attached information. Click on a particular plot to read details, such as owner and tenant.

NORTH-WEST

26 Cheshire Archives and Local Studies
Tithe maps
Price: Free
maps.cheshire.gov.uk/tithemaps/TwinMaps.aspx
View OS maps, aerial photos and tithe maps in twin windows, meaning you can zoom in and compare how the landscape has changed. You can search manually, jump to different parishes and search the apportionments data.

27 Cumbria Archives Service
Catalogue
Price: Free
www.archiveweb.cumbria.gov.uk/CalmView/FAQs.aspx
The Cumbria catalogue (launched in 2011) allows you to trawl holdings at the four county archive centres in Barrow, Carlisle, Kendal and Whitehaven. Cumberland and Westmorland wills have recently been added to the database.

28 Lancashire Archives
Police search
Price: Free
www.lancashire.gov.uk/education/record_office/records/policesearch.asp
Search for police officers with the Lancashire County Constabulary

OUT AND ABOUT
50 HIDDEN GEMS

Hull History Centre has an ongoing Second World War cataloguing project

(1840-1925), or, if your ancestor was a trader, merchant or craftsman, trawl transcripts of 27 Guild Rolls (1397-1992). 'Lancashire Lantern', meanwhile (www.lantern.lancashire.gov.uk) has an image archive and armed forces and obituaries index.

29 Manchester Archives
Burial records
Price: Free
www.burialrecords.manchester.gov.uk
The Manchester Council Archives website is very smart, and lots of its holdings are available via findmypast.co.uk. There's also a simple Online Burial Records tool, listing burial/cremation records. Searches return name, date, grave number and cemetery, but to view more details you will need to register and buy credits.

NORTH-EAST

30 Durham Record Office
Miners and light infantry records
Price: Free
www.durhamrecordoffice.org.uk/Pages/Advancedsearch.aspx
Mining Durham's Hidden Depths project created indexes to the Durham Miners' Association trade union records – currently boasting 168,207 names. Meanwhile, if you're researching a soldier, some 34,500 indexed images from the archive's Durham Light Infantry collection can be searched and viewed via the online catalogue.

31 Durham University Library
North East Inheritance
Price: Free
http://familyrecords.dur.ac.uk
This is a catalogue to more than 150,000 probate records (1527-1857) from the Diocese of Durham, covering County Durham, Tyne and Wear and Northumberland. Document images can be viewed via FamilySearch.org, and the site also provides access to Bishops' Transcripts and marriage licences.

32 Hull History Centre
Hull fishermen
Price: Free
www.hullhistorycentre.org.uk
The Hull History Centre website is notable for having particularly high-quality guides to sources. You'll find numerous practical finding aids, such as the catalogue and a PDF list of Hull-born fishermen lost at sea (c1860-2000), plus a maritime history gallery and news of its ongoing Second World War cataloguing project.

33 Leeds Library and Information Service
Photographic archive
Price: Free
www.leodis.net
The advanced search facility of this photographic archive of 52,000 Leeds images enables you to trawl by location, keyword, date or decade. You can search particular collections, such as images from West Yorkshire Archives Service. Leodis has also made 5,500 playbills from the Local Studies Library collections available.

34 North Yorkshire County Record Office
Unnetie Project Site
Price: Free
www2.northyorks.gov.uk/unnetie/search.cfm
This website currently has 10,000 historical images of North Yorkshire available to view online. You can also read about life in North Yorkshire in the past by selecting 'Storylines' from the menu, or explore interactive historic maps through the main archive website.

Portrait of Tate family outside their shop from www.leodis.net

Who Do You Think You Are? 71

Schoolchildren at Hamnavoe, from the Shetland Museum and Archives

35 Sheffield Archives and Local Studies
Picture Sheffield
Price: Free
🖳 www.picturesheffield.com
The service has an unrivalled collection of 100,000 photographs of Sheffield, recording all aspects of life in the city from the 1850s to the present day. Approximately 50,000 are available on Picture Sheffield, along with some maps. A useful tip is that holding your cursor over the image magnifies it.

36 Sunderland Register Office
BMD indexes
Price: Free to search. Certificates cost £10
🖳 www.sunderland.gov.uk/index.aspx?articleid=1399
Sunderland Register Office has made city birth (1837-2007), marriage (1837-2010) and death (1837-1970, 1985-2007) indexes available online.

37 York City Archives
Imagine York
Price: Free
🖳 www.imagineyork.co.uk
The attractive Imagine York website provides access to 5,500 digitised images from the city of York collections and those of *The Press* and *Northern Echo* newspapers.

SCOTLAND

38 Aberdeen City and Aberdeenshire Archives
PoW indexes and militia lists
Price: Free
🖳 www.aberdeencity.gov.uk/education_learning/local_history/archives/loc_aberdeenshirerecords.asp
Work continues on the digitisation of Moray Council Poor Relief Records that began in September 2011. Alongside the catalogue, you'll find local Prisoners of War Bureau Indexes (1914-1919), Loyal Volunteers of Macduff records (1795), Assessed Tax Rolls (1799-1831) and various militia lists. Aberdeen City burial records are available via DeceasedOnline (www.deceasedonline.com).

39 Angus Archives
Witches and pirates
Price: Free
🖳 www.angus.gov.uk/history/archives/resources/transcripts.htm
This page may not be much to look at, but it does include lots of free transcripts of interesting and unique items from Angus Archives. These include Forfar witch confessions, a description of a pirate attack on Arbroath in 1781 and an eyewitness account of the Siege of Mafeking.

40 Ayrshire Archives
Burgesses and Brethren
Price: Free
🖳 www.ayrshirearchives.org.uk/search.asp
This Ayrshire Archives page has two useful tools to search lists of Burgesses and Guild Brethren (1715-1920) and the Irvine Harbour Trust Harbour Book. The main site also has an online exhibition that you can browse, called 'Black History in Ayrshire'.

41 Dumfriesshire and Galloway Archives
Shipping registers
Price: Free
🖳 www.dumgal.gov.uk/index.aspx?articleid=7259
Friends of the archives have transcribed and indexed a number of key collections, including the 1851 census returns; various Kirk Session records; Dumfries jail and bail bond registers (1714-1810); and the shipping registers for Dumfries (1824-1904), Kirkcudbright (1824-1841), Stranraer (1824-1908) and Wigtown (1836-1908).

42 Fife Archive Centre
Online indexes
Price: Free
🖳 www.fifedirect.org.uk/archives
Scroll down to aids compiled by volunteers and staff that include indexes to Evacuees at Castlehill School Cupar (1939-45), miners working for the Earl of Rothes (1684-1763), Inverkeithing Public School (1884-1905), St Andrews Burgh School (1898-1909) and registers of Fife police officers from before 1949.

43 Perth and Kinross Council Archive
Perthshire militia
Price: Free
🖳 www.pkc.gov.uk/Education+and+learning/Libraries+archives+and+learning+centres/Archives
Friends of Perth and Kinross Council Archive have created finding aids that include Perthshire Militia petitions (c1704-1859), certifications (1802-1810) and papers (1680-1891). The archive holds burial registers for Perth burgh

OUT AND ABOUT
50 HIDDEN GEMS

and the Friends' database (1794-1855) gives name, age, dates of death/burial, cause of death, names of kin, occupation and details of the burial.

44 Shetland Museum and Archives
Roll of Honour
Price: Searches free, prints cost from £5.50
🖳 http://photos.shetland-museum.org.uk
A well-organised online image library with around 65,000 photographs, plus artefacts and documents from the museum's collections. Click 'Index Search' to see the wide variety of subjects that are covered. Clicking 'Roll of Honour', for example, leads to 358 well-captioned photographs of men who were killed during the Second World War.

45 West Lothian Archives
LothianLives blog
Price: Free
🖳 www.lothianlives.org.uk
Lots of archive services maintain interesting blogs, but Lothian Lives is a particularly fine example, with recent stories on Edinburgh's 17th-century poll tax (and a new index recently launched through Edinburgh City Archives – www.edinburgh.gov.uk/cityarchives), and plans of a lost chapel beneath Glencorse reservoir.

WALES

46 Glamorgan Archives
The Building of a Capital
Price: Free
🖳 www.glamro.gov.uk
Glamorgan Archives holds roughly 40,000 building regulation plans for structures in and around Cardiff city, including schools, cinemas, hotels, public houses, workhouses, hospitals, factories, places of worship and houses. This is a searchable database for Cardiff from the years between 1857 and around 1960, as well as surrounding areas from 1875 to 1926.

47 Flintshire Record Office
General index
Price: Free
🖳 www.flintshire.gov.uk/en/LeisureAndTourism/Records-and-Archives/Home.aspx
This Personal Names Index lists those in documents at the Record Office. Documents can only be viewed in person at the Hawarden office, but the index includes details such as name, location and occupation. Simply note the reference number.

48 Wrexham Council
Cemetery search
Price: Free
🖳 www.wrexham.gov.uk/english/community/genealogy/cemeteries_search/CemeteriesIndexSearchForm.cfm
This council search engine returns details of burials at the authority's main Wrexham Cemetery from 1876 to 1989. The information it provides includes name, age, place of death, date of burial, as well as the whereabouts of the individual's plot.

NORTHERN IRELAND

49 Belfast City Council
Belfast burials
Price: Free
🖳 www.belfastcity.gov.uk/burialrecords/index.asp
Provides access to a free database of burial records in Belfast from 1869 onwards, which totals around 360,000 records from the Belfast City, Roselawn and Dundonald cemeteries.

50 County Derry Genealogy Service
Derry and PRONI
Price: Free search, document access on a pay-per-view basis
🖳 www.derry.rootsireland.ie

Via this dedicated website, users can access a database of one million records, dating from 1642 to 1922, drawn from major civil/church registers of the county of Derry and Inishowen, County Donegal.

It contains pre-1922 civil birth/marriage registers, the early baptismal/marriage registers of 97 churches, memorial inscriptions from 118 graveyards and various census returns and census substitutes from 1663 through to 1901. You can search for free and view records on a pay-per-view basis. Thanks to a partnership with PRONI, you can also access the vast Derry Corporation minute books collection via www.proni.gov.uk. And of course PRONI also has several other free sources for those with interests in the area. These include the Ulster Covenant archive and Freeholders records that have also been digitised and indexed, with links to images of the original documents.

Meanwhile, a project to index/digitise 1858-c1900 wills from the District Probate Registries of Armagh, Belfast and Derry is almost complete, with the index to the will calendar entries available now.

Finally, you can also search and find scanned pages of a large number of Belfast and Ulster directories dating from 1819 to 1900.

LONDON
PIN YOUR CAPITAL ANCESTORS DOWN

Paul Blake takes you through the streets of London to uncover what your ancestors' lives were like in the big smoke

The present Greater London area occupies over 620 square miles with over seven million residents. It comprises the City of London and the 32 boroughs, 13 of which are in Inner London and 19 in Outer London. Before the creation of Greater London in 1965, the County of London covered a considerably smaller area, roughly covering what we would now call Inner London. It is this area that most people now refer to as 'London'. This County of London was itself only created in 1888, carved out of the counties that surrounded what was then the only London, the City of London itself: Middlesex, Surrey and Kent.

These historic changes have determined where the records we use to research our ancestors are kept. Importantly, when Greater London was created in 1965, the process more or less subsumed the whole of the remaining county of Middlesex. Record keeping is based on the situation immediately prior to the formation of Greater London. Therefore, the City of London and the Administrative Counties of London and Middlesex are represented by London Metropolitan Archives.

The ancient City of Westminster has its own archives. And the county record offices of Essex, Hertfordshire, Kent and Surrey are

OUT AND ABOUT
LONDON

responsible for the records relating to those areas that were taken into Greater London in 1965.

Researching London ancestors is not easy. But as more and more records are becoming available online, it is improving. The main difference between London and any other city or county is the number of inhabitants at any particular time – and the vastness of the records that were created about them.

With such a vast number of names recorded in London, even with rare ones, you cannot assume any form of relationship between one individual and another. With the introduction in recent years of huge searchable databases covering ostensibly the whole of London, or large tracts of it, searches are becoming more realistic and manageable. It is becoming less imperative to know where a family or individual was actually living at any particular time. In common with the residents of other large urban conurbations, Londoners moved frequently, usually to a new parish.

The census

The census returns from 1841-1911 are now all fully available and searchable on several websites. If London poses any particular problems not common elsewhere, they are few. Principally, it was a reasonably easy matter to not be enumerated, either by desire or accident. If you can't find your family, don't necessarily blame the commercial websites. A further problem may be the large incidence of immigrants, particularly from eastern Europe, with little English, difficult surnames and a distrust of authority – all of which caused problems when trying to record accurate information. Lateral thinking is always appropriate in any genealogical research and particularly in this case.

Parish registers, bishops' transcripts and marriage licences

One of the main causes of problems in identifying the whereabouts of a vital event in London in your family's history is the number of parishes, particularly within the 'square mile' of the City itself. Additionally, there are a few London incumbents who have yet to deposit their registers with an archive.

> Londoners moved frequently, usually to a new parish

For those used to researching in country parishes, the enormity of the registers of London churches, particularly from the early 19th century, is horrifying. For example, for the parish of St Mary Lambeth, there are in excess of 300,000 entries between 1538 and 1900. In St Pancras, there are around 1,600 burials in 1830 alone.

London Metropolitan Archives (LMA) holds the parish registers of over 800 churches within the City of London and the former counties of London and Middlesex – except for those parishes that were within the ancient City of Westminster (effectively the current Borough of Westminster). LMA has been working in partnership with Ancestry.co.uk to digitise these registers – and much other material. It is now possible to search indexed baptism registers, 1813-1906, marriage registers, 1754-1921, and burial registers, 1813-1980, online at the Ancestry.co.uk website. It is also possible to browse the composite registers of

Capital gains: were your forebears from London?

baptisms, burials and marriages pre-1812. Many, but not all, of the entries of this latter series have now been indexed. It is important to realise that this does not mean that Ancestry.co.uk offers full coverage of all extant parish registers from the City, Inner London and Middlesex.

The City of Westminster Council has awarded a contract to findmypast.co.uk to digitise ten million historic records from ▷

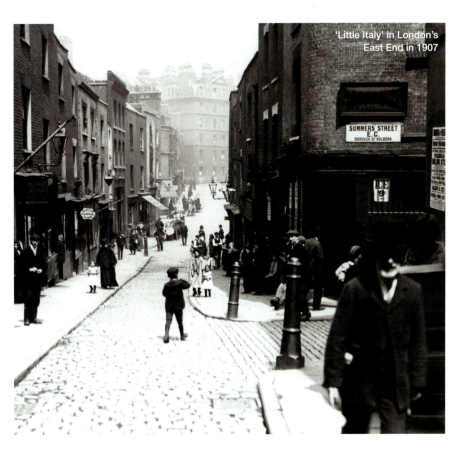

'Little Italy' in London's East End in 1907

London's poor

There is an abundance of Poor Law records for London, but the location of records created under the Old and New Poor Laws is often complicated by the fact they were designated as civil parish records before 1834 and Board of Guardians records after.

Hence they are usually separated from the religious parish records and are often to be found locally, in the borough archives rather than at London Metropolitan Archives, Westminster City Archives or the county record offices – although these do have substantial collections. Current locations can usually be determined by searching Access to Archives records at www.nationalarchives.gov.uk/a2a.

The records held at London Metropolitan Archives (LMA) are already on Ancestry.co.uk with others for the City on Origins.net; and other records on the London Lives website (www.londonlives.org). Where Settlement Certificates or Examinations survive they can be invaluable in determining the origins of an individual or family.

In the 1840s, Henry Mayhew observed and documented the state of working people in London for a series of articles in the *Morning Chronicle* – 'London Labour and the London Poor'. These were later compiled into book form in 1851 and can be read for free on archive.org.

Charles Booth's *Inquiry into the Life and Labour of the People in London* resulted from surveys undertaken between 1886 and 1903. Although it was one of several surveys of working-class life carried out in the 19th century, it is alone in that the original notes and data have survived. The final 17-volume edition was published in 1902-03.

In the published volumes, Booth chose to include only information that could be quantified – and which would not identify or embarrass any individual interviewee. For these reasons, much of the vivid detail can only be traced through use of the original notebooks.

The Booth collection, held by the Archives Division of the British Library of Political and Economic Science (London School of Economics), contains 450 original notebooks from the survey. These notebooks, together with the maps, are free to search on the LSE website (http://booth.lse.ac.uk) and give a fascinating insight into the social demography of London at the turn of the century.

Children sitting under a washing line in a slum area of London in 1889

▷ Westminster City Archives, including the parish registers – over one million of which are already online, with more to come. Although this will mean that the major collections of parish registers for London will be split between two of the major commercial companies, it is nevertheless excellent news.

It would be tempting to believe that these two resources would, between them, replace all the indexing and transcription work that has taken place over the years. For the most part, they probably will. Nevertheless, the work carried out by the Harleian Society, Percival Boyd, the Society of Genealogists, the several family history societies and many individuals and groups will continue to have a place in research – not least because some registers were destroyed or badly damaged during the Second World War, or remain with the parish.

Boyd's marriage index includes about 75 parishes but few are covered for the whole period from 1538-1837. The Pallot Marriage Index contains references to marriages from the original church registers of nearly every City parish of the established church, over 100 of them, mostly for the period 1780-1812 and some to 1837. Pallot also has a respectable covering for the Middlesex parishes in inner London, but isn't good for the Surrey and Kent parishes. Some registers, particularly City of London and Westminster parishes, have been published by the Harleian Society, but these tend to cover the earlier period only.

The collection for London on FamilySearch (www.familysearch.org), in percentage terms, is not large. Although the search mechanism is becoming increasingly clunky to use, it will continue in its importance for London research.

The difficulty of finding a marriage in London can sometimes be overcome by using the surviving records relating to marriage licences, the allegations and bonds. There were three main authorities that issued licences in London: the Bishop of London (held at LMA); the Archbishop of Canterbury's Vicar General (VG), from 1660; and the Faculty Office (FO), from 1534 (both of which are held at Lambeth Palace Library).

Indexes to the FO, 1701-1850 and the VG, 1694-1850, compiled by the Society of Genealogists (SoG), are on findmypast.co.uk. Licences were also issued by the Royal

OUT AND ABOUT
LONDON

Peculiar of St Katherine by the Tower (1686-1802), the Peculiar of the Dean and Chapter of St Paul's Cathedral (1670-1841), the Peculiar Deanery of Croydon and the Peculiar of the Dean and Chapter of Westminster, and the Archdeaconry of London (1666-91).

A Map of the Ecclesiastical Divisions within the County of London, 1903, is not available online, but can be purchased from the publisher, the London Topographical Society (www.topsoc.org) and is very useful for understanding the situation at the beginning of the 20th century.

London, like most other urban centres, attracted many kinds of nonconformist: social, political and religious. In 1821-23, it was estimated that one sixth of Londoners were nonconformist; the 1851 Ecclesiastical Census showed that only 30 per cent attended church. Many nonconformist records held at LMA are available on Ancestry.co.uk. Those to 1837, deposited with the Registrar General in the mid-19th century are available on BMD Registers (www.bmdregisters.co.uk).

Burial and cremation

Burial had always been a church function but, by the early 19th century, the burial grounds of London churches, originally laid out for small local communities, could not cope with the increasing population and high death rate. From 1852, various Acts allowed for the setting up of private cemeteries on the outskirts of the metropolis. Most passed into local authority hands during the mid-20th century with the burial registers being transferred to local borough archives.

Locating any record of a burial, particularly after the mid-19th century, is not simple. Boyd's London burials is an index to 243,000 mainly adult males from 1538-1852 and includes a large part of the nonconformist burial ground of Bunhill Fields. *The City of London Burial Index 1813-1853* covers burials from the ancient parishes within the City of London. Both are available to search on findmypast.co.uk, as is the National Burial Index, which includes some records for the London area.

Deceased Online (www.deceasedonline.com) is now making headway into the London Boroughs. This database of statutory UK burials and cremations, from the mid-19th century, currently has entries from six London Boroughs and is rapidly growing as an important resource.

Generation after generation worked at Old Spitalfields Market, shown here in 1937

Wills and probate

From 1858, all wills and administrations have been processed by the Principal Probate Registry. However, before 1858, various parts of what is now Greater London came under the jurisdiction of some 17 probate courts.

London Metropolitan Archives (LMA), Westminster City Archives (WCA), Lambeth Palace Library (LPL) and the Centre for Kentish Studies (CKS) are the main repositories and each has indexes to the wills and administrations they hold. It is essential to know what court or courts had authority where your London ancestor lived.

Indexes to many of these local courts are now starting to appear online. Findmypast.co.uk hosts the London Probate Index 1750-1858, which covers the administration of estates at nine courts. Abstracts of the Archdeaconry (to 1821) and Commissary Courts of Surrey are included in Origins National Wills Index.

Indexes to many of these local courts are now appearing online

London Signatures, on LMA's website (www.lma.gov.uk) includes an index to 10,000 wills from the Archdeaconry Court of Middlesex. Additionally, most of the original wills held at LMA – but not the register copies or other probate material – have been digitised by Ancestry.co.uk.

Importantly, many Londoners used the Prerogative Court of Canterbury (PCC) as their court of preference, especially from the mid to late 18th century. These records are held by The National Archives (TNA). The wills, but not administrations, are fully are searchable, with digitised images, on their Documents Online website: http://discovery.nationalarchives.gov.uk/SearchUI/Home/.

Directories and electoral registers

The first London directory was printed for Samuel Lee in 1677. It provided "a collection of the names of the merchants living in and about the City of London". The next London directory was the first edition of *Henry Kent's Directory* in 1734. From then onwards, directories have been published for most years. The first directory of private residents, and the first to include a streets list, was *Boyle's Fashionable Court Guide*, published in 1792. The first full street ▷

Who Do You Think You Are? 77

From 1832, electoral registers have been compiled every year, except during wartime

directory was *Johnstone's London Commercial Guide*, of 1817.

In 1841, *Kelly's Post Office Directory* (first published in 1800 and acquired by Frederick Kelly in 1836) took a form similar to its present one with the following sections: Commercial, Trades, Court (later Private Residents) and Streets.

Guildhall Library and the Institute of Historical Research both have substantial collections of directories. There are microfilm collections at London Metropolitan Archives (LMA) and Westminster City Archives. Online, you will find copies on several of the major websites, among them www.historicaldirectories.org.

Electoral registration was introduced by the Reform Act of 1832 and, since then, electoral registers have been compiled annually, with the exception of 1916, 1917 and 1940-1944. LMA holds the most comprehensive collection for the London and Middlesex areas to 1963: Ancestry.co.uk has added London Electoral Registers, 1835-1965. From 1964 LMA's collection covers the Greater London area. Other sets are to be found at county and local record offices, relevant to their own area of interest.

Prior to 1872, Poll Books listed voters at a given election only. LMA, Westminster City Archives and other local and county record offices have holdings. There is an excellent collection at the Institute of Historical Research.

Boyd's inhabitants

In 1935, Percival Boyd launched his great scheme to bring together onto 'unit sheets'

Family history societies

Get help from local experts by joining the relevant Family History Society

Greater London is covered by eight Family History Societies (FHS). Each holds regular meetings, often in more than one place within the area it encompasses, as well as issuing a regular journal. Take a look at the website of the relevant society and you will find useful information on the area and the records available, details of publications and the benefits of membership. If you join the local society serving the area where you live, even if you are not researching the area you'll be able to attend meetings, hear knowledgeable speakers and gain from the experience of the other members.

East of London Family History Society (FHS)
www.eolfhs.org.uk

East Surrey FHS
www.eastsurreyfhs.org.uk

Hillingdon FHS
www.hfhs.co.uk

London Westminster and Middlesex FHS
www.lwmfhs.org.uk

North West Kent FHS
www.nwkfhs.org.uk

Waltham Forest FHS
www.wffhs.org.uk

West Middlesex FHS
www.west-middlesex-fhs.org.uk

Woolwich and District FHS
www.woolwichfhs.org.uk

NATIONAL SOCIETIES: Here are two societies that deal with national coverage but are still particularly important and relevant to Londoners:

Jewish Genealogical Society of Great Britain
www.jgsgb.org.uk

Anglo-German FHS
www.agfhs.org.uk

OUT AND ABOUT
LONDON

basic details of family groups from all kinds of records. *Boyd's Inhabitants of London* is the best known and outside London only 34 volumes were completed. His idea was to gather together on one sheet, in addition to the dates of birth and death, residence and company of any given citizen, the names of his parents, his marriage or marriages and his children with their marriages, and a reference to his will.

No attempt was made to record grandchildren, further generations after the first having separate sheets. At the time of his death, Percival Boyd had put together a staggering 59,389 family group sheets. These are bound into 238 volumes; the index alone adds a further 27 volumes.

The collection is particularly good for 16th- and 17th-century families, although it does also include people from the 15th to the 19th century. While these can be viewed at the Society of Genealogists in London, they also form part of their collection that has been digitised and that is available to view on findmypast.co.uk.

Guilds and apprentices

By the 19th century, there were some 77 companies covering a wide range of trades. A few organisations still hold their historic records, but the majority are at Guildhall Library. A guide specifically to livery company membership records is available at www.history.ac.uk/gh/livlist.htm.

About a quarter of the Ancient Companies have records that predate 1400; about half are from before 1500. These can be in lengthy unbroken series. Records of principal interest to those seeking ancestors include: lists of members; records of entry (indentures and apprenticeship binding, freedom registers, minute books – oaths of loyalty and obedience made by those being admitted, elected or appointed); and the quarterage books, which were essentially subscription books recording membership subscriptions, due and paid, and often recording an address and date of death.

There are published histories of a large number of the great City Companies of London. Many records, most usually the earlier ones, have been re-published. In more recent years, the Society of Genealogists has published a series of London Livery Company Apprenticeship Registers. These are indexes to those registers that had not been previously published elsewhere. Helpfully, these indexes are also available on the British Origins website (www.origins.net) as 'London Apprenticeship Abstracts 1442-1850'. ■

CASE STUDY FROM THE SHOW
PATSY KENSIT

Patsy Kensit visited several London archives as she dug ever deeper into her family tree. At The National Archives, she examined the Central Criminal Court records, in which her grandfather, James Kensit, appeared with nine convictions against his name. She proceeded to Tower Hamlets Library to examine *Booth's Poverty Map* to get a sense of the dire conditions into which James had been born.

A few generations back, Patsy searched for her great great great grandfather, Thomas Kensit, in the London Post Office Directories held at the London Metropolitan Archives (LMA). She found him in Shoreditch, working as a walking stick maker, from 1857 to 1864, after which he disappears.

Still at the LMA, Patsy examined Thomas's 1815 baptism record in the parish of St Leonard's, Shoreditch, which revealed that his father Joseph was a gold beater. So it was off to the Worshipful Company of Goldsmiths in the City of London, where Patsy was shown Joseph's apprenticeship record of 1780, including his signature, and his entry in the Freedom Book seven years later. A further document in this collection revealed that Joseph's son, Thomas, later applied to the Company for financial aid, revealing that his wife Melissa was the daughter of a late clergyman.

Thus Patsy was on the trail of the Reverend James Mayne. Her journey took her to Lambeth Palace Library, where she found the Lambeth Degree Certificate awarded to James by the Archbishop of Canterbury. Further, an entry in the *Ecclesiastical Gazette* recorded his transfer from Bethnal Green to rural Buckinghamshire – a reward for 40 years of dedicated service.

FOCUS ON:
Wales

Researching your family in Wales may seem daunting, but, says **Beryl Evans**, with eight million parish registers online, you'll be tracking down your Welsh ancestors in no time…

It has always been an important part of Welsh culture to know exactly from whence you came

Wales is very much the 'Land of my Fathers'. According to the Laws of 10th-century Welsh king Hywel Dda, it was the legal duty of all to know their relatives to the ninth remove. When medieval scholar Giraldus Cambrensis travelled through the country two centuries later, he also believed that the poorest of people were able to recite six or seven generations of their family tree. Therefore, it has clearly always been an important part of Welsh culture to know exactly from whence you came.

Many of the sources used in tracing Welsh ancestors are the same in Wales as in England – parish registers, census returns and civil registration documents for example – as Wales became an administrative unit of England with the Acts of Union in 1536 and 1542.

It is often assumed that tracing Welsh ancestors is difficult, but this is not always the case if researchers are aware of the unique social, cultural, religious and linguistic characteristics of the country. One such example is the patronymic naming system prevalent in some parts of Wales until well into the 19th century.

Patronymic system
The patronymic naming system can be a challenge if you are not aware of its existence nor how it exactly works. Each man's personal name was followed by 'ab' or 'ap', meaning 'son of', then the Christian name of the father. For example, Dafydd ap Gwilym ap Rhydderch ap Thomas would reveal a string of four generations that showed Dafydd as the son of Gwilym, grandson of Rhydderch and great grandson of Thomas. In the same way, a daughter's first name would be followed by 'ferch' or 'verch', often shortened to 'vch' or 'vz', then followed by her father's Christian name.

Many of the Welsh fixed surnames are derived from personal names with the addition of an 's' – Jones, Evans, Williams and Davies for example. Others use the addition of the 'b' or 'p' from 'ab' or 'ap' to produce surnames, such as Bowen from 'ab Owen' or Probert from 'ap Robert'. Variations in spelling also need to be taken into consideration when searching early records with even the simplest of names having many variations. Rees could appear as Rice, Rhys or Reese or later with fixed surnames as Price or Pryce.

If you've ever searched for a Welsh ancestor in the civil registration indexes to births, marriages and deaths, you may be aware of the problems caused by the lack of variety of surnames in Wales: the number of records of the same name within a registration district and within the same quarter can be quite overwhelming.

This problem can often be overcome by providing the local Registrar with additional information – such as age, occupation and place of abode – to determine the correct entry within numerous ones of the same name. Certificates in Wales have always been issued in English until 1963, when bilingual certificates were made available. However, certificates are always completed in both English and Welsh or just in English.

OUT AND ABOUT
WALES

Record round-up
Track down your relatives with these records from around Wales

Nonconformist records
During the 18th and 19th centuries, Wales underwent several religious revolutions and by the 1851 Religious Census nonconformity was more popular in almost all parts of Wales than the Anglican Church. Details of where the registers have been deposited, and the periods covered, are given in Cofrestri Anghydffurfiol Cymru/Nonconformist Registers of Wales. Other nonconformist records, such as members lists, contribution books, annual reports and denominational periodicals are also of genealogical value.

Welsh newspapers and journals
The National Library of Wales (www.llgc.org.uk) has been undertaking its most ambitious digitisation project to date, which is coming to an end. Having digitised two million pages of out-of-copyright historical newspapers and journals relating to Wales, published before 1911, the library aims to launch the new free digital resource towards the end of 2012. Users worldwide will be able to search by words, phrases and dates across the collections to uncover information that would otherwise be hidden among the heavy bound volumes. This will be the largest body of searchable text relating to Wales and will contribute significantly towards realising an ambitious vision to digitise the entire printed memory of Wales.

Marriage bonds
Marriage licence bonds and allegations are an important resource for family historians. The National Library of Wales holds an online index to 90,000 records between 1616 and 1837 and hold many more (un-indexed) well into the 20th century. These records pertain to marriages that were held by licence rather than after banns. New information can be gleaned, such as age, place of abode and, occasionally, certificates of baptism.

Digitised Welsh parish registers include more than eight million records covering baptisms, marriages and burials, from 1538 onwards

Great session records
These records are unique to Wales and are equivalent to the English Assize courts. They were established after the second Act of Union in 1542 and abolished in 1830. All the original records are held at the National Library of Wales and are very under-used by Welsh family history researchers.

The Gaol Files (the criminal proceedings of the Court) have been indexed as the Crime and Punishment database. These cover the period 1730 to 1830, giving details of crimes, criminals and punishments.

Manorial records
The manorial system was not as widespread in Wales as in England and the majority of records commence in the 16th century. Substantial records can be found among the many estate records of Wynnstay, Powis Castle, Badminton, Bute, Tredegar and Golden Grove. These records are held at the National Library of Wales and other county record offices.

Finding surviving manorial records for a manor in Wales is particularly easy, as all manorial records pertaining to Wales have been recorded on The Manorial Documents Register (www.nationalarchives.gov.uk/mdr).

The register covers court rolls, surveys, maps, customs, as well as many other related records, going right up to the 20th century.

The National Library of Wales has a digitised 'Crime and Punishment' database, covering 1730-1830

Watch out!
Due to the commonality of names, surnames and place-names in Wales, it is important to record all entries in full, in order to avoid future errors by possibly following the wrong family. Tracing unusually named siblings can also help if you are stuck on a commonly named ancestor.

The Bute Docks in Cardiff, 1880

▷ The release of digitised Welsh parish registers by findmypast.co.uk includes over eight million records covering baptisms, marriages and burials from 1538. Used in conjunction with census returns from 1841 to 1911 for Wales, available via subscription websites, they can help take your research back many generations. However, the majority of registers do not commence until after 1660 and the dates covered vary from parish to parish and from diocese to diocese.

A good guide to parish register survival is the book *Cofrestri Plwyf Cymru/Parish Registers of Wales*, by CJ Williams and J Watts-Williams (National Library of Wales, 2000). As with English parish registers, those for Wales were written in Latin until around 1732 and after this date in English. You may find the occasional Welsh entry, but this is the exception rather than the rule. The original parish registers are in the custody of the county record offices.

However, the Bishop's transcripts (contemporary copies of the parish registers sent to the bishop at the end of each year) are in the custody of The National Library of Wales in Aberystwyth. Coverage of these can also be found in Parish Registers of Wales. It's worth knowing that, of the hundreds of parishes within Wales, some have not given permission for their registers to be copied and are, therefore, not included on findmypast.co.uk. A list of these is available on its website

How to search the National Library of Wales website for wills pre-1858
(www.llgc.org.uk/probate)

Step 1
Go to the search page (www.llgc.org.uk/probate) and input the information for your search – dates, name, parish etc.

Step 2
Scan the results for your search. To view the will you want, select the option that says 'Image' rather than 'Request'.

Step 3
This'll give you a digital image of the will. Move to the next pages by clicking the image number at the top of the page.

Welsh probate records pre-1858

An inventory from 1746

Wills, letters of administration and other probate records can provide invaluable information, not only for the family historian, but also for the social and local historian alike. Welsh family historians are fortunate because all the original wills proved in Welsh ecclesiastical courts before 1858 are held at The National Library of Wales, in Aberystwyth. Over 193,000 records have now been digitised and are available to search and view free of charge on its website: www.llgc.org.uk/probate.

You are able to make various searches by using the drop-down menus for 'Diocese', 'Name', 'Parish', 'Township' and 'Occupation'. A search can be made using one or all of these choices in various combinations. The main types of probate records are the will, the administration bond and the inventory. The will and inventories being the most informative. Inventories appear within the records until the end of the 18th century and can give an invaluable insight into your ancestors' lives.

It was not only the rich and wealthy that left wills and inventories. Opposite is the inventory of Mary Williams of Lisworney in 1746. It includes: "four old ordinary gowns valued at £00 08s 00d, one old and ordinary feather bed much abused by those that had ye custody of her infant daughter since her decease valued at £00 15 00".

82 Who Do You Think You Are?

OUT AND ABOUT
WALES

Top tip!
To understand better how your ancestors lived, visit some of Wales' national museums (www.museumwales.ac.uk). St Fagans, on Cardiff's outskirts, has many buildings from various periods of Welsh history, from a Victorian classroom to an early chapel, along with museums relating to Wales' main industries – coal, wool, slate and maritime.

(www.findmypast.co.uk/content/welsh-collection/parish-registers), along with a list of missing Welsh census returns (www.findmypast.co.uk/help-and-advice/knowledge-base/census/known-issues).

There are hundreds of manuscript pedigrees held within county record offices and the National Library of Wales. Descents of nobility compiled in the later Middle Ages and copied time and again have been added to by later genealogists who have donated copies of their compilations. Many of the pedigree books do not continue after the end of the 17th century, while the lack of a fixed surname and absence of place-names in the parish registers often mean that modern researchers can go no further back than the mid-18th century with any certainty.

Some of the most well-known compilations held at the National Library of Wales are the Taicroesion manuscripts by John Ellis, mainly relating to Gwynedd families, and the Alcwyn C Evans manuscripts, which relate mainly to south-west Wales. The Archives Wales website (www.archivesnetworkwales.info) is a good place to start your research, as it allows you to search the holdings of 21 repositories across Wales for pedigrees and many other collections simultaneously.

Welsh place names can cause some problems to the uninitiated, with so many Llanfihangels and Llanfairs throughout Wales. It is very important to document place-names in full and invest in a good gazetteer and familiarise yourself with place names in the area you are searching.

The Archif Melville Richards website (www.e-gymraeg.co.uk/enwaulleoedd/amr/agreement.aspx) is a place-name database that will be invaluable to researchers using Welsh records. In addition, there are useful pages relating to the Welsh language and place names at www.fhswales.org.uk. ∎

CASE STUDY FROM THE SHOW
GRIFF RHYS JONES

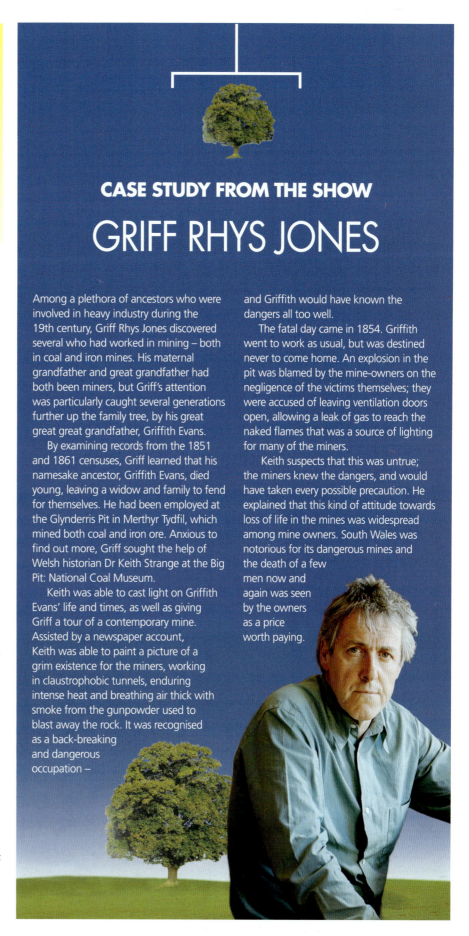

Among a plethora of ancestors who were involved in heavy industry during the 19th century, Griff Rhys Jones discovered several who had worked in mining – both in coal and iron mines. His maternal grandfather and great grandfather had both been miners, but Griff's attention was particularly caught several generations further up the family tree, by his great great great grandfather, Griffith Evans.

By examining records from the 1851 and 1861 censuses, Griff learned that his namesake ancestor, Griffith Evans, died young, leaving a widow and family to fend for themselves. He had been employed at the Glynderris Pit in Merthyr Tydfil, which mined both coal and iron ore. Anxious to find out more, Griff sought the help of Welsh historian Dr Keith Strange at the Big Pit: National Coal Museum.

Keith was able to cast light on Griffith Evans' life and times, as well as giving Griff a tour of a contemporary mine. Assisted by a newspaper account, Keith was able to paint a picture of a grim existence for the miners, working in claustrophobic tunnels, enduring intense heat and breathing air thick with smoke from the gunpowder used to blast away the rock. It was recognised as a back-breaking and dangerous occupation – and Griffith would have known the dangers all too well.

The fatal day came in 1854. Griffith went to work as usual, but was destined never to come home. An explosion in the pit was blamed by the mine-owners on the negligence of the victims themselves; they were accused of leaving ventilation doors open, allowing a leak of gas to reach the naked flames that was a source of lighting for many of the miners.

Keith suspects that this was untrue; the miners knew the dangers, and would have taken every possible precaution. He explained that this kind of attitude towards loss of life in the mines was widespread among mine owners. South Wales was notorious for its dangerous mines and the death of a few men now and again was seen by the owners as a price worth paying.

Who Do You Think You Are?

FOCUS ON:
Edinburgh

If you want to research Scottish lineage in your family tree, then getting to know the resources in the capital is where to start, says **Rosemary Bigwood**

West Princes Street Gardens, c1890 – the dividing line between the Old and New Towns

The history of Edinburgh is the story of two towns – the Old Town and the New Town. Now famous for its festivals and listed as a UNESCO World Heritage Site since 1995, Edinburgh, like many historic cities, had humble beginnings.

Traces of early settlement in the area go back to the Bronze Age. Celts, Romans and Angles all left their marks but, by the early 12th century, Edinburgh is mentioned as a king's burgh.

At the western end of a long, high sloping ridge looking out over the Forth is the dramatic Castle Rock. The Old Town stretched eastward from the castle along the hill's spine, like the skeleton of a fish, with the High Street running down towards Holyrood Abbey, and narrow closes and wynds leading off steeply either side from the main thoroughfare. At the eastern end, at the foot of Arthur's Seat round the Abbey and Holyrood Palace, another community developed as the burgh of Canongate. In 1492, Edinburgh became the capital of Scotland when King James IV moved the Royal Court to Holyrood from Stirling.

In the 16th century, the burgh was enclosed by the Flodden Wall and, as the population grew, buildings (known as 'lands') had to grow upwards – sometimes reaching 14 storeys. The town was known as 'Auld Reekie'.

After the Union of the Crowns in 1603, the Court moved to London and, in 1707, Scotland ceased to have its own parliament. But Edinburgh remained the Scottish capital and the Act of Union guaranteed the separate existence of Scottish legal courts and of the Presbyterian Church. Only in the 18th century was there a

> **During the 18th century, Edinburgh became a centre for academics**

OUT AND ABOUT
EDINBURGH

Edinburgh Castle, home to displays and museums

gradual emergence of a new era for Scotland and its capital. Internal peace after the Battle of Culloden, together with the economic advantages of union with England encouraged trade. Wealth and population grew.

In 1752, proposals were presented to drain the Nor' Loch – a malodorous stretch of water below the north side of the High Street, later to become Princes Street Gardens – and to build on the higher ground beyond it. In 1766 James Craig's plan for the New Town was accepted – a grid system of streets running east and west (Princes Street, George Street and Queen Street) linked by cross streets, with gracious squares at the east and west ends. The New Town is now accepted as one of the finest examples of Georgian architecture worldwide.

Merchants, gentry and professional men moved from cramped housing in the Old Town to the space and grandeur of the New Town. During the 18th century, Edinburgh became a centre for philosophers, scientists, economists and academics of all kinds.

Edinburgh, although overtaken by Glasgow in size, remains the capital of Scotland, the seat of its parliament and a centre of financial services, tourism and culture. With its fine museums, archives and libraries, this is the place to start to explore the history of Scotland and to find out about past generations who lived there.

Four essential places to visit

1 SCOTLANDSPEOPLE CENTRE

✉ HM General Register House,
2 Princes Street,
Edinburgh EH1 3YY
☎ 0131 314 4300
🖳 www.scotlandspeoplehub.gov.uk

ScotlandsPeople Centre is in the historic General Register House at the east end of Princes Street, close to Waverley Station. ScotlandsPeople is known through its pay-per-view web facilities, but a visit to the centre is very worthwhile – as TV presenter Monty Don found out in his recent episode of *Who Do You Think You Are?*.

All of the 'foundation' genealogical records for the whole of Scotland are available to search. A daily fee of £15 gives unlimited access to statutory registers of birth, death and marriage from 1855 onwards, census returns 1841-1901 (1911 will be released in 2011), old parish registers (the earliest go back to the 16th century), minor records including some consular returns, divorce registers and deaths at sea, as well as the Public Register of All Arms and Bearings in Scotland from 1672 onwards – there is a 100-year closure.

Indexes and images of Scottish wills and testaments up to 1901 can be viewed without extra charge (for post-1901 wills, go upstairs to the National Archives Historical Reading Room). The library also has useful reference books, including a great many recorded monumental inscriptions.

Free two-hour 'taster sessions' for newcomers are run twice a day at the centre and, for an additional fee, assisted searches provide personal help in adding branches to family trees. These can be hugely rewarding and an enormous amount can be found in a day's research. What is uncovered and established will provide the basis for further research elsewhere. ▷

The inside of the Adam Dome, ScotlandsPeople Centre

Watch out!

There are some vital differences between Scotland and other parts of the UK. Scotland has retained its own legal system, affecting many aspects of life, and particularly legal records – in inheritance, land ownership and the court administration. Gaelic (mostly only spoken now in the West Highlands) is the national language of Scotland.

2 NATIONAL ARCHIVES OF SCOTLAND

✉ HM General Register House,
2 Princes Street,
Edinburgh EH1 3YY
☎ 0131 535 1314
💻 www.nas.gov.uk

Under the 1707 Act of Union between England and Scotland, it was agreed that the records of Scotland should "continue to be keeped as they are within that part of the United Kingdom now called Scotland". But it was not until 1774 that Robert Adam began designing Register House to house the Scottish archives. Records can be consulted in the Historical Search Room at the archives, but many are outhoused and need prior ordering.

The enormous range of source material can be overwhelming, but this is a treasure trove of material relevant to the whole of Scotland – most of which is not online – going back to the pre-1707 Scottish government. This rich haul covers records of nationalised and other industries, legal records including deeds, sasines (transfers of land) and trade and tax records, as well as records of courts and testamentary material.

The NAS holds other invaluable resources – collections of estate papers, maps and plans, church records and many records of the burghs. Time spent exploring this archive will be well-rewarded.

A growing number of key records are now digitised and can be searched without charge in the Historical Search Room. These include Established Church records for the whole of Scotland, records of dissenting churches, testaments and wills dating back to the 16th century. Work on digitising sasines and valuation rolls is ongoing.

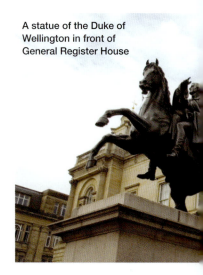

A statue of the Duke of Wellington in front of General Register House

3 NATIONAL LIBRARY OF SCOTLAND

✉ George IV Bridge,
Edinburgh EH1 1EW
☎ 0131 623 3700
💻 www.nls.uk

For the family historian, there is a wealth of valuable information on Scotland's history and culture here in the country's largest library, founded in 1925.

For those with Indian connections, there are reports of police and of medical institutions, on military matters and civil administration. There are accounts of emigrants and background information about the conditions they experienced and collections of official publications including parliamentary reports, too. The library also collects copies of every Scottish newspaper, going back to the 18th century.

Among the collections are papers on Scottish labour history, documents on Scots abroad, on missionary work in Africa and many acquisitions of Scottish estate papers, which are rich in family information. The National Library of Scotland Maps Reading Room is housed in a separate building 15 minutes walk away.

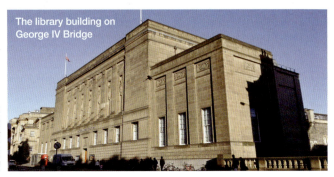

The library building on George IV Bridge

4 EDINBURGH CITY ARCHIVES

✉ Level 1, City Chambers,
High Street, Edinburgh EH1 1YJ
☎ 0131 529 4616
💻 www.edinburgh.gov.uk

If your ancestors lived or worked in Edinburgh, a visit to the city archives may be very rewarding. As a royal burgh, Edinburgh had rights of self-government and was entitled to elect a council, admit burgesses, organise the incorporated trades, hold courts and look after the poor.

The Canongate, an area located outside the old city walls in the lower part of the Royal Mile, was a separate burgh whose records are also in the archives. They cover all aspects of life and include fascinating collections of historical records of local businesses, societies and persons, as well as visual materials such as postcards and photographs.

There are many army and militia registers (mostly

OUT AND ABOUT
EDINBURGH

unindexed) covering the 18th and 19th centuries, records of workhouses and Parochial Board poorhouses, minutes of school boards, records of some schools and details of trials and imprisonment of criminals, as well as some police records.

Registers of a number of Edinburgh's Episcopal congregations are also held here, including baptisms, marriages and burials, rolls of congregations and minutes.

For an overview of the archive's holdings, check the Scottish Archive Network website at www.scan.org.uk and search under Edinburgh City Archive code – GB236. ∎

CASE STUDY FROM THE SHOW
DAVID TENNANT

The ScotlandsPeople Centre in Edinburgh is a magnificent resource for those starting out on their Scottish family history research, and its visitors have often included members of the *Who Do You Think You Are?* research team.

The centre boasts, among other records, indexes and copies of birth, marriage and death certificates from 1855, and census returns from 1841-1901. These records, many of which are also available remotely on the centre's website www.scotlandspeople.gov.uk, have been the cornerstone of many a genealogical investigation, not least for actor David Tennant when on the trail of his mother's McLeod ancestors.

It was in the 1861 census that David caught his first glimpse of Donald McLeod, his great great grandfather, living with his wife and children in Glasgow and working as a humble labourer. But David learned from this census return that Donald had not been born in the city: his place of birth, much to David's surprise, was listed as Kilminion on the Isle of Mull. Thus David was launched on a journey to the remote Scottish village where his ancestors had lived as cotters. It was a journey that linked his family to one of the most momentous events of Scottish history – the Highland Clearances.

He was able to locate and visit the church in which Donald and his many siblings had been baptised in the early 19th century – and even the ruins of the village in which they had lived before the Clearances came in 1814. Not bad from the information provided on a single census return!

FOCUS ON:
Dublin

If you have Irish ancestors, then this guide to the capital's research hotspots is essential for planning your trip, says **Sarah Warwick**

Trinity College and the Bank of Ireland in Dublin, c1897

In May 1988, the Dublin Millennium 50 pence piece was made legal tender in Ireland, in recognition of the city's 1,000-year anniversary. This was convenient, for coin-makers, if incorrect; a continuous settlement had existed on this site for hundreds of years before then.

However, the modern city might be said to have been born around 988AD, when the rule of invading Norse Vikings gave way to that of homegrown High Kings of Ireland and the city was given its Celtic name, Baile Átha Cliath, meaning 'town of the hurdled ford'.

Much of Dublin's early history was an ongoing battle between three rival groups – the Norman-Vikings, Danes and the local Irish. Anyone visiting the city to research their family's history will find that this pattern of instability has been repeated down the ages.

Family historians visiting Dublin find a pattern of instability down the ages

After the Danes were ejected in the Middle Ages, the city settled into relative tranquility, but the calm only lasted until the next invasion. From across the Irish Sea in 1649, Oliver Cromwell stormed the country, sacking cities that resisted his control and leaving behind a new term for evil-doers, with Irishmen calling them simply 'Cromwells'. His suppression and disenfranchisement of Ireland's papist population, and enforced Protestant settlement, sowed the seeds for later troubles.

British rule

While under British control, Dubliners were subject to every whim and action of Parliament. Although many of these were unpopular, the Wide Streets Commission of 1757 had a very positive effect on the city, spearheading

OUT AND ABOUT
DUBLIN

urban regeneration and brightening up the old slums.

As a result, thousands of people poured into the region and, for a while, the Georgian city was the second largest in the British Empire. The immigrants benefitted from Dublin's new industry, including shipping, business and the factory of Arthur Guinness at St James's Gate, which, having been set up in 1759, would grow to become the city's largest employer.

Alas, the good days were not to last and the 19th century was a dark time for Dubliners. The Act of Union of 1800 meant that the seat of government had moved from Dublin Castle to Westminster. Dublin had little to offer the Empire in terms of industry and so entered a long decline, with thousands leaving to find work. The population dwindled further during the famine of the 1840s, with more than a million people dying and the same number emigrating to more promising lands.

Early 20th-century conflicts brought destruction upon the city, with the Easter Rising of 1916, the Anglo-Irish War and the Irish Civil War resulting in the loss of many lives, buildings and records (including most of the 19th-century census returns).

Since Ireland's independence, almost a century ago, the city has gradually been restored to its glory days. The final years of last century were very prosperous, resulting in a renewed period of immigration, increased business and economic growth, at least until the banking crisis in 2005.

If you want to trace your Irish ancestors, but don't know where to begin, just follow our guide to all the best resources.

Church Street in the aftermath of the Easter Rising in 1916

Four essential places to visit

1 NATIONAL ARCHIVES OF IRELAND (NAI)

✉ Bishop Street, Dublin 8
☎ + 353 (0)1 407 2300
🖥 www.nationalarchives.ie

Ireland's main repository – the NAI – is housed in the old Jacob's biscuit factory in the former slum area of the Liberties. As well as holding the jewels of the country's archive collection, the building played its own part in the history of the Republic when it was one of the garrisons held by rebels during the 1916 Easter Rising.

It's home to a formidable gamut of resources. Most useful for genealogical research, of course, are the censuses, although these are incomplete following the great fire at the Four Courts in 1922. The NAI has the complete returns for 1901 and 1911 (both are searchable online), and the surviving fragments for 1821, 1831, 1841 and 1851, which are pretty paltry.

There are also various 'census supplements', including the original documents from the Griffith's Land Valuations, Tithe Applotment Books from the 1820s and 30s, voters' registers, and Church of Ireland parish records on microfilm.

Also useful are the collections of genealogical abstracts, donated by people who were family historians before 1922, which include census information for hundreds, if not thousands, of individuals.

The highlight of a visit here will be a free assessment from the in-house team of the Association of Professional Genealogists in Ireland (APGI) staff, who will be able to suggest a plan of action and might even be able to help you take your research back to the Middle Ages. ▷

The NAI houses the surviving census returns and other collections

Watch out!

Aideen Ireland, head of reader services division at the National Archives of Ireland, says: "People must come prepared. The three things they should check before they come are BMDs (from 1864 onwards), parish records and wills. Now that the 1911 census is online, they should use that too."

2 NATIONAL LIBRARY AND GENEALOGICAL SERVICES OFFICE

✉ Kildare Street, Dublin 2
☎ + 353 (0)1 603 0200
🖥 www.nli.ie

The National Library of Ireland's impressive Victorian building

The National Library of Ireland's (NLI) handsome Victorian building is a prime destination for Irish research. The main genealogical holdings of the NLI are the Catholic parish records, which can fill in the gaps left by the absence of census returns. These are on microfilm, searchable by area and date but there's no surname index (one does exist at the Irish Family History Foundation website, usable for a fee: www.irish-roots.ie).

Computers in the library's genealogy service have free internet access for searching the 1911 census records or Griffith's Land Valuations online. Also, subscriptions to a number of other online resources are available, from the Irish Times Digital Archive and 19th-century British Library Newspapers to old Irish Ordnance Survey maps.

Other records of value to researchers in the genealogy collections are land valuations, trade and social directories, estate records and newspapers, which are all available to browse freely in the genealogy centre. There's also the manuscript collection, which visitors need a readers' ticket to access (the genealogy collections are accessible without one) and will need a more concerted effort to use. Estate papers, lists of tenants, voters' lists, trade and street directories: all of these can be a great help.

Sources at the library include the digitised search tool (http://sources.nli.ie), which is a comprehensive online index for finding any mention of someone or somewhere across huge swathes of the collections, all accessible just by typing a name or keyword.

3 GLASNEVIN MUSEUM

The ashes-containing columbarium wall at Glasnevin Cemetery

✉ Glasnevin Cemetery, Finglas Road, Dublin 11
☎ + 353 (1) 882 6590
🖥 www.glasnevinmuseum.ie

Opened in April 2010, Dublin's genealogy museum has been hailed as a gift to local researchers, with its displays on family, social and local history. The museum is the official exhibition space for Glasnevin Cemetery, Dublin's largest burial ground – home to 1.5 million of the city's dead.

Tours of the cemetery are run seven days a week – €6 (€5 concessions). These have long been popular with visitors to the city, and often top guidebook lists of the city's most unusual or underrated activities.

Visitors to the museum can now delve further into the story of the 180-year-old 'Irish Necropolis', with the museum's permanent exhibitions on famous internees and Irish burial and death practices.

There's also a database of all those buried here so you can search for your own ancestor. Museum admission is €6 for adults and €5 concessions. A cheaper combined ticket, covering both museum and cemetery, are available.

More on the people buried at Glasnevin (as well as Dardistown, Newlands Cross and Palmerstown cemeteries, plus Glasnevin and Newlands Cross Crematoriums) can be found at www.glasnevintrust.ie/genealogy.

OUT AND ABOUT
DUBLIN

4 GENERAL REGISTER OFFICE

✉ Government Offices, Convent Road, Roscommon
☎ + 353 (0) 90 663 2900
🖥 www.groireland.ie/research

Located in the Life Centre, just north of the Liffey, the General Register Office is the place to come to search Irish BMD indexes. Its research facility, on the third floor, is open every weekday (excluding public holidays), 9.30am-4.30pm.

Indexes that are searchable here include those for Irish births, marriages and deaths that took place anywhere in Ireland from 1864-1921, as well as those for all events that took place in the Irish Free State/Republic since 1922, and Legal Domestic Adoptions registered in Ireland from 10 July 1953 onwards.

Searches can be undertaken on an individual basis (it costs €2 for a specific search of any five-year period) or more generally (€20 a day for a wider search). Photocopies of all records can be obtained for €4 a copy.

The office does not have the records for Irish-born citizens who died abroad – these are held at the main GRO in Roscommon and can be obtained directly from there (tel: +353 (0) 90 663 2900).

Also in the Life Centre is the Valuation Office, which collates and holds information relating to property in Ireland. Its archives go back to 1850 – useful for tracing house history or finding out more about a forebear's home. ■

A Free State soldier patrolling the streets of Dublin during the Irish Civil War

CASE STUDY FROM THE SHOW
DERVLA KIRWAN

Dervla Kirwan visited several Dublin repositories during the course of her research. For her mother's side, she went to the Military Archives at the Cathal Brugha Army Barracks to view the pension file of her grandfather, Finian Collins O'Driscoll, a prominent IRA member and nephew of the legendary Michael Collins.

These records are not usually open to the public, but an exception was made for Dervla. Through them, she discovered that Finian joined the IRA in 1920 aged just 17 and was involved in intense, highly risky guerrilla warfare.

On her father's side, Dervla investigated her great grandfather Henry Kahn. Beginning at the Irish Jewish Museum, she met the curator who provided a copy of Henry's naturalisation records. These revealed that he had fled persecution in Russian Poland in about 1880, worked as a tobacconist and had five children. Moving on to the General Register Office, she collected his marriage certificate, confirming that he had married a Catholic in a Protestant church.

The National Archives of Ireland holds both records of the Irish Jewish community and historic newspapers, which between them revealed a prison sentence for Henry following a likely miscarriage of justice.

Dervla then visited the atmospheric Kilmainham gaol, where Henry was detained, and the Richmond District Lunatic Asylum, now St Brendan's Hospital, where psychiatrist Brendan Kelly provided her with Henry's admission records. Such institutions hold their own records and others have deposited them in local or national archives, so make sure you check what is available and where before you visit.

Butcher, baker, candlestick maker?

It's not all about births, deaths and marriages. **Pam Ross** explains how investigating your ancestors' working lives can reap rewards

The building trade, shown here in Lowry's 1932 painting *Excavations At Manchester*, employed many casual journeyman workers

OCCUPATIONS
CIVVY STREET

For ordinary people through the ages, there's always been a very fine line between earning enough to feed the family and falling into poverty. Many crossed this line several times during their lifetime.

In 1842, Patrick Hughes, a calico printer told a commission into child employment that "work just now is very slack; there are numbers unemployed. I have to support my mother, my brother, who is sickly, and my mother in law, as well as my own family. I am therefore obliged to put my children to work."

When work was "very slack", ordinary employees were not paid and had to rely on family and friends or, if they were lucky, payments into a providence or social fund. For everyone, even the most successful, the fear of 'ruin' was always there – and the threat of the workhouse loomed large.

Although it became normal, particularly in the 20th century, for some workers to stay with one employer all their lives, many British workers were hired by the day. Ranked between master and apprentice, came the 'journeyman', hired for a day's work. Also, agricultural labourers would go where they thought there would be seasonal work, often walking long distances, and if they were not taken on that day they would have another long walk to look for more. There was no money for the periods they did not actually work.

There were enlightened employers like Cadbury and Lever who housed and educated their workforce but the fact that their names are still remembered highlights how rare they were. In the main, job security, and with it the health and welfare of whole families, depended solely upon the goodwill, if not the whim, of the employer.

Women, in theory, gave up work when they got married. In practice, in poorer families, they carried on working but that work went largely unacknowledged and unrecorded by official documents. Women were often simply identified by the job their father or their husband did. Death certificates, for example, usually described a woman as 'wife of' or 'widow of'; on marriage certificates the space for a wife's occupation was often left blank.

So where to look for information about occupational records?

Finding occupational records
The names of some of the jobs our ancestors did are still recognisable today, but others need more research to find out what the job actually involved. There are online and printed lists available aimed at family historians and the longest version of the *Oxford English Dictionary* is a good source. Googling an unusual job title can often bring results. Once you've discovered what the job was, what then? Can you find out more?

The answer in many cases is 'yes', but be prepared to work hard at it. Try to start your search armed with as much information as you can – date of birth, where they lived and when, likely dates of employment, date of death – because you will be lucky if you find an index to help you. Did they do a clerical job or did they work on the factory floor or its equivalent? Were they members of a union? All this information might help you to narrow your search once you have located any surviving records.

> **Trade directories are available at various fee-charging websites**

The majority of records of business are held in local and county archives, university archives or with individual companies if they still exist. For former nationalised industries, try The National Archives (TNA) at Kew in south-west London.

Trade & professional directories
If your ancestors were in business on their own account, trade directories can tell you where they were in trade and for how long. The directories are mostly divided into county volumes containing entries for specific towns and villages. Take into account the fact that it could take up to two years for the companies, such as Kelly's and Pigot's, to physically collect and publish the information. Even then, the information gathered was usually limited to a name, address and occupation.

Professional directories are specific to a particular profession, such as the Law Lists for members of the legal profession or *Crockford's Clerical Directory* for Church of England clergymen. The amount of information each of these gives varies, but you can sometimes uncover a year of birth or the date of joining the profession, along with details of various appointments.

Trades and professional directories are available at the various fee-charging websites, but you will need to look around in the first instance to see who holds exactly what. For example, Ancestry.co.uk and FamilyRelatives.com both offer a selection of medical registers. You can also find directories at larger libraries and archives. Some are free online at www2.le.ac.uk/library/find/specialcollections. ▷

A poster depicting the cotton industry from 1927

Who Do You Think You Are? 93

▷ Apprentices

Not everyone served an apprenticeship and not all apprenticeship records have survived. A large number have now been indexed – but not all in one place.

Pauper children were often apprenticed by their parish, so that they would not be a drain on local resources. The records of these apprenticeships are usually in county and local archives. Apprenticeship indentures can give details about the apprentice's age, parish and parents and the master's trade and parish.

You can also get a good idea from the agreement of what was expected of the apprentice and what was offered by the master. Other apprenticeships came about through a private agreement with the family of the child. Papers regarding private apprenticeships may have survived in local archives in solicitors' collections.

For about a hundred years after 1710, many apprenticeship indentures were subject to payment of a tax. The Society of Genealogists (www.sog.org.uk) has an index to these taxed agreements (1710-1774), now also available at findmypast.co.uk. The original documents are held at TNA in Kew.

City of London livery companies kept records of their Freemen and apprentices. These cover a wide range of trades and skills, including goldsmiths, apothecaries and grocers. Some have been indexed at Ancestry. co.uk. The London Metropolitan Archives is now the first port of call for enquiries about City Apprenticeships. For Guilds outside London, try local archives.

Qualifications

Members of the professions often appear in volumes of university alumni; (for instance, *Alumni Oxonienses* lists Oxford graduates). The earlier copies give details of a person's age and career, with information about their father. Oxford and Cambridge are often available in libraries, with some copies online (visit www.archive.org for a selection of free digitised copies). You might have to search a bit harder for other universities, except within their local area, but the Society of Genealogists has a good range. For modern university yearbooks, enquire first at the university itself.

When civil servants sat their entrance exams (or applied for a pension), they had to produce documents to verify their age. Again, the Society of Genealogists has an index to the small percentage of these documents that have survived, from 1752 up to the 20th century. The index is also available at www.findmypast.co.uk.

A blacksmith in his foundry, next to his anvil and forge, c1905

Trade union records

Warwick University Modern Records Centre (www2.warwick.ac.uk/services/library/mrc) has a large collection of trade union records, which include the Transport and General Workers' Union and the National Union of Railwaymen. The Centre has online research guides, including a useful list of occupations and the trade unions most likely to apply (from bricklayers to bookbinders).

As well as membership records, if you're lucky you may find details of benefits paid

Pension records can tell a lot about a person's working life

out on injury, illness or death. The website explains what is available that may be of interest to family historians and what you need to know in order to access the records; for instance, the date of death or the name of the union branch that the person being researched joined.

Disciplinary records

You might find a note of a disciplinary offence in a wages book and then want to look further. Offences might have been more fully written up in Caution Books with details of the offence committed, such as "leaving the works without permission" or "failing to take duty as booked".

You might also find details of any punishment – perhaps a fine docked from their wages or a suspension. The final sanction was, of course, dismissal and, if there was a house that came with the job, for example, in the case of miners or railway workers, then this meant that the spectre of homelessness would be an additional consequence.

A small number of Railway Company Caution Books are online at Ancestry.co.uk. Any surviving for other companies will be found via the National Register of Archives (www.nationalarchives.gov.uk/nra).

Staff registers, appointment and wages books

These are well worth looking for, but these records' survival is patchy. Staff registers for the old railway companies are at TNA, with some available on Ancestry.co.uk, where you can also access appointment books for Royal Mail (if you do find someone who worked for the Royal Mail, it is well worth visiting their archive).

Staff records of the Royal Household are available on findmypast.co.uk. The bare minimum of information you should find will be the name of your ancestor and the job they did. There can also be columns for date of birth, date of employment, rate or grade of pay and date of (and possibly reason for) leaving.

If your ancestor was dismissed, rather than leaving for a long and happy retirement, it will usually say so. If you are lucky, you might find the reason noted as well.

OCCUPATIONS
CIVVY STREET

A transportable cider press at use in Somerset in 1934

Understanding your ancestor's occupation

Even if you can't locate details of your forebear's working life, you can get an idea of their profession

Once you've uncovered what your ancestor did for a living, then you can at least find out more about their occupation – even if you can't uncover many personal records. Start by reading up on the local history as some occupations were common to a particular area (for instance, mining, needle making, weaving) and there might be photographs and descriptions of how people worked.

Sometimes the best books are long out of print and have to be searched for on the shelves of local libraries. Once you have found a useful book, keep a watch on eBay or abebooks.co.uk in case a copy turns up. It's also worth checking Archives.org. For more, visit websites devoted to a specific area, for example, Digital Handsworth (digitalhandsworth.org.uk) or The Glasgow Story (theglasgowstory.com).

Many local libraries and archives now have sound archives and some of these include interviews that focus on a particular occupation. Somerset Archives, for example, has made some of its oral histories available online at www.somersetvoices.org.uk/people. Cider-makers, blacksmiths, farmworkers and a cricket bat maker are among the people interviewed. The British Library has a large collection of sound archives including an oral history section. A few of its recordings are available online at http://sounds.bl.uk/Oral-history.

And don't forget moving pictures. The British Pathé website (www.britishpathe.com) offers many clips of people at work, while the British Film Institute's collection, including intriguing documentaries on coal mining and London's East End docks, can be viewed at the BFI in London, as well as centres elsewhere in England (see www.bfi.org.uk for details). Sample clips from their collection can be seen on www.youtube.com/user/BFIfilms.

Seek out the published diaries and memoirs of people who worked in the same occupation as your ancestors, like Jennifer Worth's *Call The Midwife*. Novels can also help. Elizabeth Gaskell's *Mary Barton*, published in 1848, gives a flavour of the lives of mill workers in Lancashire, and Thomas Hardy's *Tess Of The D'Urbervilles*, published in 1891, is a reminder of the insecurity of agricultural work.

Pick an occupation or place relevant to your family's history and visit one of the 'living museums' dotted around the country. The Highland Folk Museum at Newtonmore, the Ulster Folk and Transport Museum, Beamish Living Museum, the Black Country Museum in Dudley and the Historic Dockyard in Chatham are just a few of them. They all offer demonstrations of some of the old skills and working methods used by our ancestors.

Staff and union magazines

Some union magazines can give a good view of what the main concerns of the workers were at the time your ancestor was in employment, as well as containing names of some members. However, it helps to have dates and subjects of possible searches – such as an accident or a strike, if you are looking for an individual.

The same applies to staff magazines. These can be very good for photographs of retirement presentations, awards given or works outings, but you have to have a good idea when the retirement might have taken place – or when the award been won – in order to avoid a long search. If a company has lodged its archive with the local record office, you should check to see if staff magazines are included.

It is difficult to read union and staff magazines without being drawn into the articles about people's working lives. Even if you find nothing about your ancestor, it won't be time wasted.

Pensions

Any employment that came with a pension was prized. Pension records, when available, can tell a lot about a person's working life because some detail was needed to confirm their entitlement to a pension. Files can give date of birth, occupation, rate of pay and name and address of next of kin. Not everyone qualified for a pension. For example, the only Post Office employees entitled to a pension were senior staff, at least until the rules changed in 1860.

Pension records for members of the Armed Forces are at TNA, with some online at Ancestry.co.uk and findmypast.co.uk. Like other documents containing personal ▷

Top Tip

The business your ancestor worked for might still be in existence under another name. Mergers and takeovers could have meant several changes of company name. Trade and telephone directories can be a help. Companies House offers a free online search for previous names over the past 20 years at www.companieshouse.gov.uk.

CASE STUDY FROM THE SHOW
SHEILA HANCOCK

If your ancestor worked for a particular company, it is always worth finding out if its archive survives, as it may enable you to discover more about this ancestor's life and experiences.

Sheila Hancock knew that her grandfather, George Thomas Hancock, had been employed by Thomas Cook and a visit to the company's archives produced an 'agreement book' listing George as an 'agent' in Milan. The archivist explained that this was a lofty position, equivalent to a branch manager, and that someone must have seen potential in George to promote him to this station. George would have guided the great and the good around the sites of Milan.

Further, a staff magazine from May 1927 carried a photograph of George along with his retirement notice. Elsewhere, the minutes of a company meeting discussing the possibility of introducing staff pensions proved to Sheila that George would not have benefitted, explaining why his widow was unable to maintain the lifestyle to which she had grown accustomed.

Company archives may contain all kinds of gems: staff lists, wage books, company rules, magazines, advertising material and a great deal more. Often the archivist will be an expert in the company's history and able to put your findings into context.

Teacher registrations from England and Wales can be viewed at the Society of Genealogists as well as findmypast.co.uk

▷ details, all pension records might be subject to restrictions of anything up to 100 years.

Licences
Some occupations, notably running a public house or working as a gamekeeper, required a licence. Applications to Quarter Sessions for these licences are held at local record offices and archives in England and Wales. Some have been indexed and some published by both archives and family history societies.

Teachers in England and Wales were also licensed. Their licences came from the Bishop of the Diocese in which they taught and were recorded in Act books. If these survive, they are likely to be in Diocesan Archives (often, but not always, these are the same as county archives). The Society of Genealogists (www.sog.org.uk) has records of nearly 100,000 teacher registrations from 1914-1948 which can be viewed for free by members or accessed for a fee from www.findmypast.co.uk).

Estate papers and farm records
A high proportion of our ancestors worked on the land. Many worked as agricultural labourers for yeoman farmers and landed gentry. While many of the documents have gone, some do remain – in particular, those relating to larger estates. Wages books can be found and payments to skilled craftsmen brought in for a particular job were also recorded.

Some documents might still be with the family. Others are likely to be in County Record Offices or specialist archives like the Museum of English Rural Life at the University of Reading.

Accounts books can give you the names of workers, what they were paid, when they were taken on and when they left.

OCCUPATIONS
CIVVY STREET

There might be farm diaries that include more than the bare facts relating to stock and harvests, and personal diaries and letters. Even if you do not find anything relating specifically to your ancestor it is worthwhile looking just to get a flavour of the kind of life your agricultural ancestors led.

Records of large estates can be spread between several archives and catalogued under different names. It is useful to know the names of the landowners and tenant farmers, and the area they farmed. Local history books and trade directories will give you the names of principal landowners and some farmers.

A search of the National Register of Archives will give you an idea if there is anything available for a particular estate or landowner. Alternatively, a call to the county or local archives should set you on the right path.

Indexes

There are a number of privately owned indexes relating to particular professions. Some of these are advertised online and some through family history societies. Genuki (www.genuki.org.uk), for example, gives access to an index of British Coastguards, 1841-1901. Privately run websites, such as the Waterway index via www.canalmuseum.org.uk, can contain not only names but valuable information on working conditions.

Accident reports and factory inspections

Life as a porter for the Great Western Railway was obviously hazardous, and mishaps like "Churn fell on foot" and "Foot injured by trolley wheel" were recorded by companies in their own 'accident books'.

By 1833, the government had recognised that legislation was needed to protect people from accidents at work. The Factories Act laid down safety measures and appointed four

> *Farm diaries might include more than just stock and harvests*

factory inspectors. Their reports have been published in book form and include detailed accounts of their visits and names of some individuals. The British Library has copies, and larger institutional libraries and archives often have copies available or extracts relating to their area. A few appear on free book websites such as Archive.org.

Inspectors of Mines were similarly appointed and some of their reports on mining accidents have been quoted on websites, such as The Scottish Mining site (www.scottishmining.co.uk) and The Coalmining History Resource Centre at www.cmhrc.co.uk. Reports include a description of the circumstances of the accidents and sometimes the names of those who died.

The sites also feature extracts from the detailed reports of the Children's Employment Commission, 1842. This was set up to investigate the working conditions of children and includes interviews with both children and adults. Origins.net has published one of the reports free online, with a breakdown of some of the occupations covered.

Their work, their lives

Searching for occupational records can take quite a lot of time. If they have survived at all, they might be spread across two or more different archives. You might have to travel some distance and then, in the end, find nothing relating directly to your ancestor. However, simply by looking through the records that do survive, you can learn a great deal about your ancestors' working world and the concerns that preoccupied them. ■

TAKE IT FURTHER

➡ *Researching Your Family History* by Pam Ross (The Crowood Press, 2010)

➡ **www.reading.ac.uk/merl** The Museum of English Rural Life archive, based in Reading

Finding company archives

STEP 1:
Search the National Register of Archives (www.nationalarchives.gov.uk/nra), home to details of 32,000 business records and 108,000 organisations. Search by organisation or land-owning family. The ARCHON directory gives details for libraries and archives mentioned (www.nationalarchives.gov.uk/archon).

STEP 2:
For nationalised industries, check TNAs' catalogue (www.nationalarchives.gov.uk/catalogue). They also hold Board of Trade Files of Dissolved Companies, containing samples of records from failed businesses. Chancery records include some business documents submitted in evidence and never reclaimed.

STEP 3:
If the first two steps seem impossible because you have too little information, try a general search at TNA's Access to Archives (A2A) www.nationalarchives.gov.uk/a2a. Genuki also has links to occupational sources at www.genuki.org.uk/big/Occupations.html.

Who Do You Think You Are?

The Merchant Navy comprises ships from many different shipping companies

Researching the Merchant Navy

Janet Dempsey steers you safely through the choppy waters of tracing Merchant Navy ancestors, with a guide to The National Archives' holdings

If you have an ancestor who served in the Merchant Navy, there are plentiful resources at hand. The website www.findmypast.co.uk holds 1.25 million employment record cards (1835-57 and 1918-41) relating to hundreds of thousands of merchant seamen and women. These indexes have previously been available on microfiche at The National Archives (TNA), while the original cards are held at Southampton City Archives.

The Merchant Navy is not a single entity or service in the same way as the Royal Navy is, and comprises ships from many shipping companies – from giants such as Cunard and P&O to individual fishing boats owned by the captain. Early 20th-century seamen who served aboard British Merchant shipping were required to register with the Registrar General of Shipping and Seamen (RGSS) and it is those records that are now available.

In addition, the Master's Certificates collection, digitised in partnership with the National Maritime Museum at www.ancestry.co.uk, features a diverse range of documents recording people who applied to qualify as merchant seamen between 1850 and 1927.

OCCUPATIONS
MERCHANT NAVY

Shifting fortunes
During the 19th century, the British Merchant Navy was the envy of the world but, in the years that followed, the Merchant Navy experienced very mixed fortunes and ultimate decline. Ships, along with their crews, were requisitioned for First World War service and these bore the brunt of Germany's policy of unrestricted submarine warfare – its men and ships endured heavy losses.

It was also a major player in the golden age of the liner, when transatlantic travel was used by the rich and famous for pleasure, and by emigrants from Europe looking for a new life in the United States. Merchant Navy seamen and women provided the stewards, maids, boot boys and laundresses, as well as the firemen and the able seamen, for these boats.

But many of these employees suffered dreadfully during the Great Depression, when mariners would sign on to a ship for the duration of a voyage only and would be out of work again when that trip was over. During this period, such was the shortage of work that shipping lines were signing men of officer rank to do jobs normally filled by ordinary seamen.

In 1939, the Merchant Navy was again called on to serve its country during the Second World War. Its losses were relatively high compared to the other armed services; over 30,000 merchant seamen were lost in the conflict.

Supplementing the records
Aside from the employment record cards held at www.findmypast.co.uk and www.ancestry.co.uk, there are numerous other online and paper records that can supplement your searches. The amount of information available for any given period varies enormously. For example, if your ancestor served from 1900-1918, you will need to know the name of at least one ship he or she served on, as no records ▷

Is your relative one of these seamen?

CASE STUDY FROM THE SHOW
LAURENCE LLEWELYN-BOWEN

Laurence Llewelyn-Bowen knew his maternal grandfather Ronald Wilks had a nautical past and so visited his uncle Christopher to find out more. Christopher showed Laurence his father's Seaman's Discharge book that contained vital information to Ronald's time in the Merchant Navy. Laurence learned that he'd joined the Merchant Navy at just 17 and his first ship, the *Kohistan*, sank during the First World War.

Pursuing this line of inquiry, Laurence visited The National Archives, where official reports into the sinking of Merchant Navy vessels are held. He discovered that the *Kohistan* was in convoy with two Royal Navy ships, travelling a perilous route from Burma to Gibraltar. The National Archives revealed minutes of a court of inquiry into the sinking, revealing that the *Kohistan* was sunk by a German U-boat.

Seeking first-hand testimony of these harrowing events, Laurence headed to the Imperial War Museum. There he found the diary of Herbert Wilde, commander of the Royal Navy escort. Wilde's writings reveal he felt helpless when the ship was hit and blamed the drunken captain of the other escort vessel. The court of inquiry had declared that no-one was at fault for the incident, that it was just a "misfortune of war".

Laurence then headed to Germany and spoke to U-boat expert Oliver Meise at the Bundesarchiv in Freiburg. The diary entry of the commander of the UC-35 confirmed that the U-boat was tailing the *Kohistan* above water, but wasn't spotted. Then it opened fire.

Laurence was relieved to discover that none of the 30-strong crew perished in the attack. "It must have been a really, really scary experience."

Who Do You Think You Are?

▷ for individual seafarers were kept by the RGSS from 1856-1913. RGSS records dating 1913-1920 were destroyed years later.

If you have the name of a ship on which your ancestor served, see 'The next steps to take – searching by ship', below. If you do not have a vessel name, you can consult the index compiled by the Crew List Index Project (CLIP) available on findmypast.co.uk. This list, covering the period 1860-1913, details all the seamen named on crew lists and agreements held by county records offices, but does not include the crew lists held by TNA or those transferred to the Maritime History Archive in Newfoundland, and so represents about ten per cent of surviving crew lists.

Merchant seamen were issued with medals for the First World War. They were awarded the Mercantile Marine Medal if they served at sea for more than six months between 4 August 1914 and 11 November 1918. Additionally, they were awarded the British War Medal if they served at least one voyage through a danger zone. The cards, in series BT 351, that detail the award of these medals are available to download from www.nationalarchives.gov.uk/records/medals.htm. They do not give a lot of personal detail beyond date and place of birth, but if the medals were sent to a home address, then that is usually given.

For service between 1918 and 1921, the record series BT 350 are available through findmypast.co.uk. The series was created by an order made under the Defence of the Realm Act and is a record of ID certificates issued to merchant seamen. The real bonus of these records is that the vast majority contain a photograph – and they also usually list at least some ships a seaman served on.

Ships' records

From 1921 to 1941, the RGSS kept two card indexes that are now record series BT 348 and BT 349 (also now on findmypast.co.uk). BT 349 is CR1 cards, alphabetically arranged by surname and giving date and place of birth and discharge number (please note that a Merchant Navy discharge number is given at the start of service, not at the end, and reflects the fact that a seaman is continuously discharged from ships). It will also give a brief physical description of each individual, as well as

The SS *Lusitania* was torpedoed by the Germans in May 1915

The next steps to take – searching by ship

If you're fortunate enough to have found details of your forebear's ships, where should you go next?

Once you have a service record that lists the ships your ancestor served on, it is time to build on this information. Ships' masters were required to provide a crew list for all voyages and this gives details of how seamen were employed on board. Crew lists from 1861 onwards are very dispersed, with the vast majority held at the Maritime History Archive in Newfoundland. Its website allows you to search by ship number and, if it holds the document, you can apply for a copy. If it doesn't have the record, you can search The National Archives' catalogue with the ship's official number, using the reference BT 99 – or by ship's name if it is a 'celebrated' ship under reference BT 100.

For the Second World War period, you may need to do additional searches under reference BT 380 and BT 381. The National Maritime Museum at Greenwich holds the majority of crew lists for years ending in '–5', except for 1945. The remaining holdings are dispersed throughout county records offices.

In 1939, the Admiralty issued an order that merchant vessels were not to record destinations or ports of call in log books or on crew lists. Instead, a centrally held card index of ships' movements was produced. This is now available online through The National Archives' Discovery facility and is searchable by the name of the ship.

In addition, The National Archives' catalogue additionally allows you to search for convoy numbers for the Second World War if you have this information.

The Merchant Navy was called upon during the World Wars and suffered heavy casualties

OCCUPATIONS
MERCHANT NAVY

Being a merchant seaman was a dangerous profession, especially during wartime

indicating any distinguishing marks. Some cards also have a photograph of the seaman.

The second of these card indexes is the CR2 cards in series BT 348. These are arranged numerically by discharge number and list the ships the seaman served on (usually by the ship's official number) and the date the seaman signed on to the ship's crew.

It is possible to find out the name of a ship from the ship's number – remember that while a ship's name can change, its number never does. You can search this via TNA's catalogue and several record series are now being catalogued by ship's name and number. You can also try the CLIP website www.crewlist. org.uk. Click on 'Finding aids', then 'Ship by official number' and simply type in the number of the ship.

Although the records from the fourth register cover only the first few years of the Second World War, it is possible to take your research further. Medals were issued to Merchant Seamen but, unlike for the First World War, seamen had to apply and prove their movements while at sea. Records of medals awarded are available at TNA in record series BT 395, also available via the Discovery facility. Queries about medals outstanding should be directed to the Maritime and Coastguard Agency.

From 1941 to 1972, the RGSS changed the way it kept records for merchant seamen. Two series exist: the seamen's pouches, which contain loose documents and sometimes a photo ID, and are held in series BT 372, BT 390 and BT 392. Records of employment

> "Remember: a ship's name can change, but its number never does"

on form CRS 10 are docket books listing all ships served on, employment details, date and place of signing on, date and place of discharge, and details of conduct and ability.

Other avenues

Being a merchant seaman was a dangerous profession; loss of life was high. If your ancestor was unfortunate enough to have lost his life at sea during the 20th century, you can trace this through the records in BT 334. Gallantry Awards to Second World War merchant seamen are in series T 335 and are searchable via the online catalogue by name of recipient or name of ship.

There is also a wealth of information about merchant ships in the Admiralty records, particularly ADM 137 for the First World War and ADM 199 for the Second World War.

All of these records are held at TNA. They are original documents and will require you to visit Kew. You will need to obtain a readers' ticket; details of this, and ID requirement, can be found on the website. Staff in the reading rooms will advise you on accessing the records.

Finally, enquiries for Merchant Navy records post-1972 should be directed to the Maritime and Coastguard Agency (www. dft.gov.uk/mca). ■

TAKE IT FURTHER

➜ **www.nmm.ac.uk** The online home of the National Maritime Museum in Greenwich

➜ *Tracing Your Merchant Navy Ancestors* by Simon Wills (Pen & Sword, 2012)

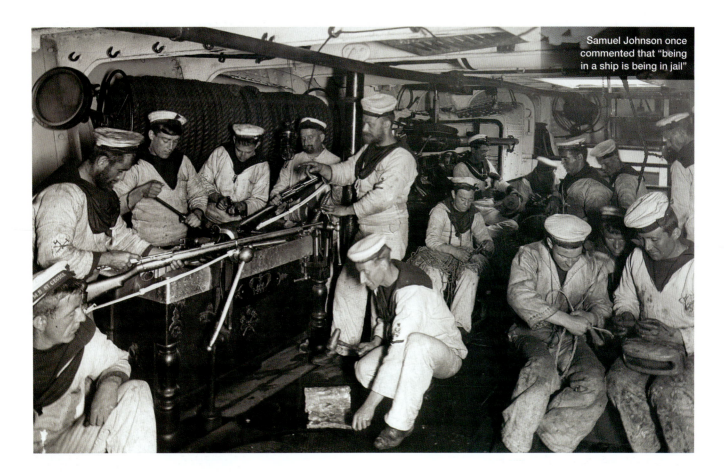

Samuel Johnson once commented that "being in a ship is being in jail"

Royal Navy ancestors

Naval records can provide invaluable personal, career and social information about an ancestor's life. **Janet Dempsey** makes sense of the paper trail

Being the oldest of Britain's armed forces, the Royal Navy is known as the Senior Service. As well as holding that distinction, it was also the most dominant navy in the world for most of the 18th and 19th centuries. British history is studded with famous naval victories – the Armada, Trafalgar and the Battle of the Nile – and Admiral Lord Nelson is the epitome of an Englishman doing his duty to the last.

However, beneath the veneer, the Navy was a harsh employer, laying off men in their thousands during times of peace and using impressment (recruiting men by force) during times of emergency. Discipline and conditions were hard, as expressed by 18th-century English essayist Samuel Johnson who wrote: "No man will be a sailor who has contrived enough to get himself into a jail; for being in a ship is being in jail, with the chance of being drowned. A man in a jail has more room, better food and commonly better company."

The Royal Navy was also a substantial employer and in 1810 alone, it had in its employ more than 140,000 men.

It is, therefore, of little surprise that many family historians find they have naval ancestors on their tree. Researching Royal Navy forebears is both popular and stirs the imagination.

The roots of the modern Royal Navy are firmly planted in the Tudor age with the creation, by Henry VIII in 1546, of the administrative body that was to become the Navy Board. However, it fell into disrepute and was linked with scandal under the Stuarts. It was later reformed by a man more famous for his diary than his career at the Admiralty – Samuel Pepys. The foundations were laid for a Navy that embraced professionalism and new advances in science and seamanship, and would go on to became the world's greatest.

With the Royal Navy being such a huge and important employer, there is more than a fair chance that you have a Royal Naval ancestor. Look for clues in census returns and birth, marriage and death recordsIf you think you have a Royal Navy ancestor, then you

OCCUPATIONS
ROYAL NAVY

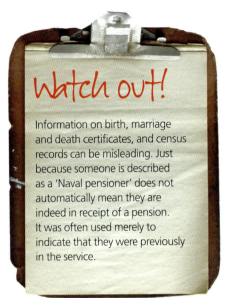

Watch out!
Information on birth, marriage and death certificates, and census records can be misleading. Just because someone is described as a 'Naval pensioner' does not automatically mean they are indeed in receipt of a pension. It was often used merely to indicate that they were previously in the service.

need to determine whether he is an officer, warrant officer or rating (non-officer level seaman). The way that the Admiralty kept the records for officers and ratings was completely different, so you could save hours of fruitless research by establishing your forebear's rank before you start looking for him in the records.

A word of caution, though – the titles associated with ranks have changed over time and you might need to consult the publication *Tracing Your Naval Ancestors* by Bruno Pappalardo for a comprehensive list.

However, as a rough guide, commissioned officers include admirals; commodores; captains; commanders; lieutenants; mates; masters (from 1808); surgeons (from 1843); pursers (from 1843); chaplains (from 1843); naval instructors (from 1843); engineers (from 1847); midshipmen and naval cadets.

Among the job titles included under the category of warrant officers are boatswains; gunners; carpenters; engineers (1837-1847); chaplains (until 1843); artificer engineers and school masters.

Most common among the Ratings (although there are hundreds more) are able seaman; coxwain; blacksmith; cook; bandsman; stoker; yeoman; petty officer; chief petty officer; signalman; ropemaker; sailmaker; steward; shipwright; caulker and leading seaman.

On the right path
The first place to check if you are unsure about your ancestor's capacity is the Navy List. Sets are available at The National Archives (TNA) and the National Maritime Museum, as well as at larger libraries. It lists officers who are serving in the Navy, but who are not ratings. It follows, therefore, that if ▷

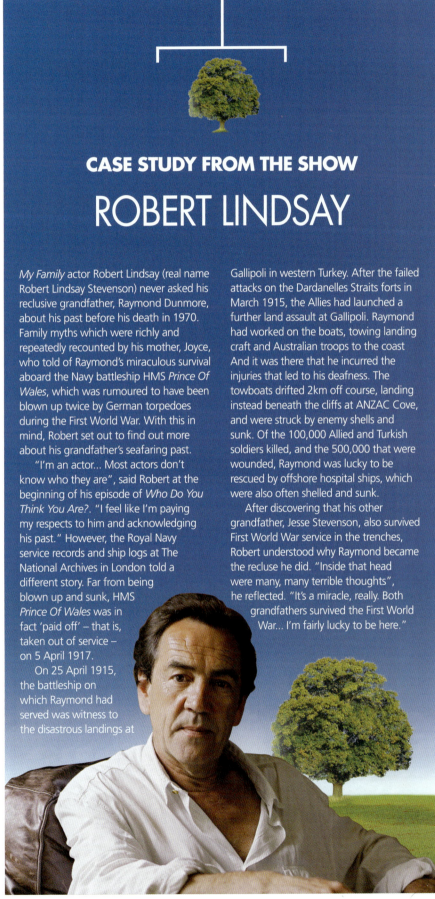

CASE STUDY FROM THE SHOW
ROBERT LINDSAY

My Family actor Robert Lindsay (real name Robert Lindsay Stevenson) never asked his reclusive grandfather, Raymond Dunmore, about his past before his death in 1970. Family myths which were richly and repeatedly recounted by his mother, Joyce, who told of Raymond's miraculous survival aboard the Navy battleship HMS *Prince Of Wales*, which was rumoured to have been blown up twice by German torpedoes during the First World War. With this in mind, Robert set out to find out more about his grandfather's seafaring past.

"I'm an actor... Most actors don't know who they are", said Robert at the beginning of his episode of *Who Do You Think You Are?*. "I feel like I'm paying my respects to him and acknowledging his past." However, the Royal Navy service records and ship logs at The National Archives in London told a different story. Far from being blown up and sunk, HMS *Prince Of Wales* was in fact 'paid off' – that is, taken out of service – on 5 April 1917.

On 25 April 1915, the battleship on which Raymond had served was witness to the disastrous landings at Gallipoli in western Turkey. After the failed attacks on the Dardanelles Straits forts in March 1915, the Allies had launched a further land assault at Gallipoli. Raymond had worked on the boats, towing landing craft and Australian troops to the coast And it was there that he incurred the injuries that led to his deafness. The towboats drifted 2km off course, landing instead beneath the cliffs at ANZAC Cove, and were struck by enemy shells and sunk. Of the 100,000 Allied and Turkish soldiers killed, and the 500,000 that were wounded, Raymond was lucky to be rescued by offshore hospital ships, which were also often shelled and sunk.

After discovering that his other grandfather, Jesse Stevenson, also survived First World War service in the trenches, Robert understood why Raymond became the recluse he did. "Inside that head were many, many terrible thoughts", he reflected. "It's a miracle, really. Both grandfathers survived the First World War... I'm fairly lucky to be here."

The types of records held...

...and what you can find out from them

The National Archives (TNA) is probably the best source for the records of Royal Navy ancestors.

▼ Officers

The Navy Lists *(1782-present)*
The first place to check for officers' records is the Navy List. This is available at TNA as well as other libraries and archives around the country. The New Navy List, an unofficial publication between 1841-1856, gives some biographical information too.

Registers of Officers' Service *(1756-1966)*
The registers of service were only really kept in a systematic fashion from 1840. Now being digitised, these records are available via Documents Online.

Returns of Officers' Service *(1817 and 1846)*
The Admiralty sent out surveys for serving officers to complete and return to the Admiralty in 1817 and 1846. A warning: not all surveys were completed or returned.

Officers' Passing Certificates
These series contain details of certificates issued to officers who'd passed various examinations to ascertain their suitability for a particular rank or role. They provide information about a man's service prior to examination, and sometimes include other papers such as certificates of baptism.

▼ Ratings

Any man who served at Trafalgar is now recorded on the Trafalgar Ancestors Database – www.nationalarchives.gov.uk/trafalgar.

Continuous Service Engagement Books *(1853-1872)*
Men entering the Royal Navy after 1853 were given a Continuous Service (CS) number. Many of these records are searchable via Documents Online. These list the date and place of birth, a physical description and a summary of service.

Registers of Seamen's Service *(1873-1923)*
For each man, these records give a date and place of birth, former occupation, a physical description and a list of the ships he served on.

▼ Warrant officers and ratings

Applications *(1802-1894)*
These records detail service in support of applications for a naval pension or admission to Greenwich Hospital. They give a record of ships and dates served and the total time served in the Navy.

▼ Using ships' names...

Ships' Musters
These useful registers will list the entire crew of the ship and, from 1764 will usually provide extra personal details of the crew members, including age and place of birth. From around 1800, description books can be included with the musters and will give a physical description of the man.

Ships pay books
These can be used to confirm a man's service on board a particular ship.

Ships' allotment registers
Royal Navy men and officers were often away from their families for months or even years at a time. To help ease the hardship of such families whose main breadwinner was away so much of the time, the Royal Navy introduced a system of payments home that were called allotments. Such payments were recorded in large ledgers and are accompanied by a wealth of information, including the next of kin. These registers are being catalogued, to search by either ship or inidividual, as part of an ongoing project at TNA.

▼ Resources

➡ TNA has a whole series of **Research Guides** to help you plan your research.

➡ They are free to download and print from here: www.nationalarchives.gov.uk/catalogue/researchguidesindex.asp?WT.lp=gs-researchguides

➡ The **online catalogue** can be searched via www.nationalarchives.gov.uk/catalogue/search.asp

➡ **Documents Online** is available via www.nationalarchives.gov.uk/documentsonline/navy.asp

A Navy sailor's years of service can be illuminated through research via The National Archives

Occupations
Royal Navy

Wrens filled a range of crucial roles

Women's Royal Naval Service

Searching for relatives in the armed forces you'll see war wasn't just a man's game. Tens of thousands of women saw service in the ranks of the Wrens…

The first Women's Royal Naval Service (WRNS, popularly known as Wrens) was a short-lived affair lasting from November 1917 to October 1919. There were many men filling shore-based roles, which were deemed suitable for women to fill while the men went to sea. Its creation was therefore "to free a man to join the fleet".

At first, Wrens took over the cleaning, cooking and stewarding jobs, but later took on more specialist roles, such as electricians, dispatch riders and wireless operators. The selection criteria for Wrens was set very high, meaning that many women did not meet the standards required. Although they were subject to strict rules of conduct, they were not, however, subject to the Naval Discipline Act. The total number of Wrens who served during the First World War was 438 officers and 5,054 ratings. The Wrens were reformed in 1939 and the service reached its peak – 74,620 – in 1944.

Familt historians should be aware that officer ranks for Wrens serving during the First World War included director, deputy director, assistant director, deputy assistant director, divisional director, deputy divisional director, principal, deputy principal and assistant principal. Officers' records can be found at The National Archives in record series ADM 318, also available via DocumentsOnline at www.national archives.gov.uk/documentsonline. Here you can search by an individual's name and download the complete record.

There are also two registers in ADM 321 that detail appointments, promotions and resignations for Wrens officers between 1917 and 1919.

As with the officer ranks, ratings titles were deliberately chosen as to sound as unlike military ranks as possible. Non-officer Wrens were described by the job they did, so look out for cooks, cleaners, typists, telephone operators, clerks and the such like within the records. They are described as 'Mobile' or 'Immobile'. Wrens who were mobile could be posted around the country and even abroad; Those who were immobile remained at one base.

Details of service are held in record series ADM 336 and are also available on Documents Online (www.nationalarchives.gov.uk/documentsonline). The Engagement papers and an archive of photographs, artefacts and oral histories are held by the Royal Naval Museum (Portsmouth PO1 3NH) and are are available to view by appointment – call 023 9272 7562 and ask for the curator of the Wrens collection.

Service records for those who served after 1956 are held by the Ministry of Defence, NPP (Acs) AFPAA Centurion Building, Grange Road, Gosport PO13 9XA. You need to be next of kin to access them.

▷ your ancestor is in the list, then you follow the path to find an officer and if he is not, then you need to look for a rating.

However, a further complication needs to be considered – service in the Royal Marines. Royal Marines served on board His/Her Majesty's ships alongside Royal Navy sailors. Royal Marines officers' records are kept with Royal Navy officers' records; however, Royal Marines other ranks are not kept with ratings records.

If a particular division is mentioned in the information you have about your naval ancestor (that is, Plymouth, Portsmouth, Woolwich, Chatham or Deal), then it is likely you are looking for a Royal Marine rather than a Royal Navy rating.

The Royal Navy did not keep personnel records in any systematic fashion until 1840 for officers (available in the ADM 196 series at TNA) and 1853 for ratings (ADM 188). Records after these dates are largely available at Documents Online www.nationalarchives.gov.uk/documentsonline, simply search using your ancestor's name or other known data.

It is possible to trace records of those serving earlier than these dates, but for earlier periods you need to know the name of a ship that your forebear served on (you may find this by consulting TNA cataloguing projects).

As an example, a search of the 1881 census reveals James John Dempsey serving as a stoker on board HMS *Monarch* aged 24. We know he is Royal Navy personnel because of the 'HMS' prefix to the ship. And we also know, from the list on page 103, that his job means that he's a rating.

However, a quick check of the Navy List confirms this. A search in ADM 188 on Documents Online brings up the name James John Dempsey, aged 24. When the document is downloaded, it shows that the service record is for a stoker who was born in 1856 and was indeed serving on board HMS *Monarch* from 1878 until 1892.

For further examples on records that can help you with more detailed research, see the guidance on Navy Genealogy at The National Archives. ■

TAKE IT FURTHER

➡ **The Fleet Air Arm Museum** The Somerset museum holds Royal Navy engagement registers

➡ **The Caird Library** Based at Greenwich's National Maritime Museum, this holds lieutenant's log books from 1673-1809

Who Do You Think You Are? 105

Just because First World War records aren't online, it doesn't mean that they don't exist

Find British Army records

If you want to track down each and every record of your army ancestors, you may need to leave your computer behind and head off to The National Archives at Kew. **Simon Fowler** is your guide

Most people researching their family history will come across someone who fought in the army at some point in their family's past. Conscription wasn't introduced until the First World War, so the army had relied on volunteers. Pay was regular, though poor, and until the 19th century you signed on for 20-25 years, so it tended to attract the less wealthy. A pension at the end – and an initial Bounty – helped. The army kept records of soldiers because of money. Muster Rolls confirmed who was with a Regiment so pay could be checked. Discharge Papers confirmed how long, which regiment and where he served, so pensions could be calculated.

Most family history researchers come across soldier ancestors by finding them listed as Pensioner or Chelsea Pensioner in a 19th-century census; sometimes recorded as a soldier on their marriage or death or at a child's birth.

The officer, usually coming from wealthier classes, frequently purchased his Commission. Though some officers made a professional career of it, many served for only a few years – but were subject to recall in the event of war.

Officers' records were kept by both their regiment and by central government and there were occasional reviews of their circumstances. Because promotion depended to some extent on length of service

OCCUPATIONS
ARMY

Watch out!
Unlike other army units, the five guards regiments (that is the Coldstream, Grenadiers, Irish, Scottish and Welsh guards) still keep their own service records. If your forebear was in one of these, you will need to contact the appropriate headquarters at Wellington Barracks, Birdcage Walk, London SW1E 6HQ.

('seniority') they appear in the regularly produced (annually early on, then monthly) Army List and their promotions are also recorded in *The London Gazette*.

Luckily, there are plenty of websites that offer advice, information and records that will help you research your British Army ancestors. Surviving First World War service records can be found at Ancestry.co.uk, while many pre-WW1 records can be found at www.findmypast.co.uk. The National Archives has also put a selection of military records available online.

However, one of the common pitfalls family historians fall into is to assume that, because the records aren't yet online, they don't physically exist. This is particularly true with army records, where only a small proportion are online.

Army records are largely to be found at The National Archives (TNA) at Kew. You will either have to go in person to use the material or find somebody to do the work for you. If you decide to do the research yourself, you will probably be looking through original documents, so you'll need to obtain a reader's ticket. Full details of doing this are given on TNA's website (www.nationalarchives.gov.uk), which also has a number of excellent research guides that can help you understand what you are looking at.

At present, you can search online (at Ancestry.co.uk or findmypast.co.uk) for service records for men who served in the army between roughly 1760 and 1920. But these records are not complete. Two-thirds of service documents for men who served during the First World War were lost in the Blitz. Before 1913, the only documents that have survived are those for men who received a pension. If a man died while in the army or deserted, as so many did, there is nothing. ▷

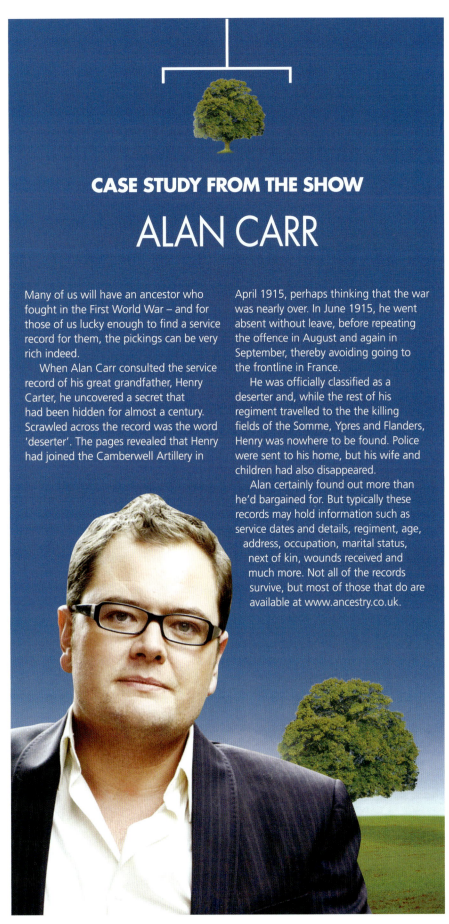

CASE STUDY FROM THE SHOW
ALAN CARR

Many of us will have an ancestor who fought in the First World War – and for those of us lucky enough to find a service record for them, the pickings can be very rich indeed.

When Alan Carr consulted the service record of his great grandfather, Henry Carter, he uncovered a secret that had been hidden for almost a century. Scrawled across the record was the word 'deserter'. The pages revealed that Henry had joined the Camberwell Artillery in April 1915, perhaps thinking that the war was nearly over. In June 1915, he went absent without leave, before repeating the offence in August and again in September, thereby avoiding going to the frontline in France.

He was officially classified as a deserter and, while the rest of his regiment travelled to the the killing fields of the Somme, Ypres and Flanders, Henry was nowhere to be found. Police were sent to his home, but his wife and children had also disappeared.

Alan certainly found out more than he'd bargained for. But typically these records may hold information such as service dates and details, regiment, age, address, occupation, marital status, next of kin, wounds received and much more. Not all of the records survive, but most of those that do are available at www.ancestry.co.uk.

Who Do You Think You Are? 107

Other avenues worth pursuing

The National Archives isn't the only place that may have information about soldier forebears. Other museums and archives have something to offer

▼ National museums

There are two national museums which have large collections of private papers, photographs and other material for the British Army. These are the National Army Museum, which collects material about the Army in general, and the Imperial War Museum, which concentrates on the wars of the 20th century. The National Army Museum specialises in the Indian Army and also has material for the Irish regiments and the East Kent Regiment.

There are online catalogues so you can check out what material they have, although neither are complete. Both museums have fascinating galleries where you can get a feeling for the life that your forebears had in the army.
National Army Museum, Royal Hospital Road, London SW3 4HT; Tel: 020 7730 0717, www.nam.ac.uk
Imperial War Museum, Lambeth Road, London SE1 6HZ, Tel: 020 7334 3922, www.iwm.org.uk.

▼ Regimental museums

These are a good source if you are researching officers or senior non-commissioned officers. Their holdings vary considerably, but you might expect to find collections of personal papers and photographs, copies of war diaries, regimental magazines and registers and records, which TNA, for one reason or another, did not want.

Regimental magazines, which begin to be published in the 1890s are particularly interesting, describing battalion activities, promotions, sports days and the like.

The Army Museums Ogilby Trust provides details about individual regimental museums at www.armymuseums.org.uk.

▼ County record offices

A number of regimental museums have deposited their archives in regional archives, where they can be properly looked after and catalogued. Regiments which have done this include the Durham Light Infantry, the Queen's West Surrey, and Bedfordshire regiments.

And while you're thinking locally, regional/city/town newspapers may well contain stories about soldiers and the activities of local units, such as the annual manoeuvres or the award of gallantry medals to local men.

The National Army Museum in London

▷ Nor are there any records for officers yet online, although you can build up a rough idea of an officer's service from *The London Gazette*, which can be found online at www.gazettes-online.co.uk.

The other resource online is medal rolls – and their equivalent for the First World War, the Medal Index Cards. They are complete for both officers and soldiers but are not generally very informative.

Yet there are masses of records about officers and ordinary soldiers that have yet to be digitised, particularly if your forebears were in the army before 1914. And in some cases they never will be copied. The Victorian and Edwardian army was famous for its bureaucracy, which is good news for family historians because there are masses of registers and rolls to look through.

You can also uncover more about what a unit did in a particular campaign or action by reading regimental and general military histories or, for the First and Second World Wars, you can look at War Diaries. These describe in detail what the unit did day by day, whether it was taking part either in the big push or in the regimental sports day.

TNA is planning to put its set of First World War diaries in series WO 95 online by 2014. TNA also holds hundreds of books about various wars and individual campaigns, which can help interpret the military experiences of your ancestor.

The officer corps

Officers made up about ten per cent of the strength of the army. They lived very different lives to the men they commanded and this is reflected in the records. Details of promotions and the regiments to which a man belonged can be found in the Army Lists. These were published four times a year. A complete set is in the Open Reading Room at TNA and many regimental museums and libraries will also have sets.

There's also the unofficial *Hart's Army List*, published between 1838 and 1915, which includes biographies of many officers that will tell you in which campaigns they fought. In fact, these are arguably the most useful records available.

Until the First World War, the army did not maintain central records for officers; instead this was largely done by individual regiments. This means you will need to know which regiment your officer served with. If you are not sure, the Army Lists should tell you.

Promotion ledgers

There isn't a single series of service records, nor a single document describing an officer's

OCCUPATIONS
ARMY

Indian Army records can be found at the British Library and the National Army Museum

service. Instead there are ledgers containing details of promotions in series WO 25 and WO 76. Fortunately, there is a card index in the Open Reading Room that will make life easier, telling you which registers to look at for your man.

Officers held their rank by virtue of a royal commission. Before 1871 they could be bought and sold. There are some fascinating papers at TNA about this in the Commander-in-Chief's Memoranda (series WO 31) covering the period between 1793 and 1870.

As well as applications, they include supporting documentation, such as statements of service, certificates of baptism, and letters of recommendation. These papers are arranged by the dates when the event was announced in *The London Gazette*, the date is also given in the Army List.

Before 1871, men who wished to retire either sold their commissions, recouping their capital investment, or went on to half pay. Half pay indicated that, in theory at least, officers were available to be recalled to their regiment in time of war.

There are several series of registers at Kew (series PMG 3- PMG 14) listing officers on half pay, which will give you your ancestor's address and regiment, as well as indicating when he died. After 1871, there are similar – but again, rather uninformative – registers indicating payments of pensions, both to the officer or to his widow and children if he died while on service.

During the First World War, files were kept on individual officers. They are now at Kew in series WO 339 and WO 374 with an index available through TNA's online catalogue.

Officers lived very different lives to the men they commanded

The contents of files vary considerably and are fullest for those who were killed in action. But you should expect to find papers about an ancestor's enlistment, promotions and particularly concerning payments of pension or allowances.

Other ranks

If you can't find your 'other ranks' forebear in the service records online (or even if you can), there are several series of records at TNA that can fill in the gaps. However, these records are arranged by regiment, so you have to know which unit your forebear served with.

The most important of which are Muster Rolls (series WO 12-WO 16), which begin in the 1720s and go up to 1898. These record the payment of wages and allowances (as well as money taken to pay for food, uniforms, etc) to individual soldiers and officers month by month. There are generally four muster rolls a year.

They also indicate when and where a man enlisted (sometimes giving his place of birth and birth date) and when, where and how he was discharged – or in army jargon, "became non-effective". Again, a place of birth may be given. Muster rolls will also indicate where a man was away from his regiment on detachment, promotions and demotions. From 1868, they may tell you about wives and children in married quarters.

You probably won't want to go through each roll, as the information often does not change from year to year. But try to find the ones that record when he joined and left, and possibly check every fourth or fifth one.

Description Books

Another set of records to look out for are Description Books (series WO 25), which give a description of each soldier (with colour of hair and eyes, plus any distinguishing marks), his age, place of birth, trade and service.

They were compiled so that, if a man deserted, something which was very common until the 1860s, descriptions could easily be sent out to the police. The books themselves are in alphabetical order of soldiers' names. They date between 1756 and 1900, but for most regiments the books stop in the 1850s.

The chances are that soldiers would have been court martialled at some stage during their career, usually for drunkenness, disobedience or desertion. Generally they appeared before district court martials (series WO 86), where records begin in 1829 and go up to the 1970s.

If your forebear received a pension (and if you have a service record for him, then he did), then it is worth checking out the Pension Admission Books (series WO 116-WO 118 – not yet online). They exist for the Royal Hospitals in Chelsea and Kilmainham (for Irish soldiers) and are arranged by when the soldier applied for a pension, which was generally when he left the army. They will provide name, rank, age, total service, rate of pension, foreign service/stations, character report, place of birth and trade. Later volumes will indicate which medals he was awarded. ■

TAKE IT FURTHER

➡ *Tracing Your Army Ancestors* Simon Fowler's book on the subject, published in 2008

➡ www.nationalarchives.gov.uk/archon
Describes all British archives with weblinks

WHO DO YOU THINK YOU ARE?

SUBSCRIPTION ORDER FORM WDBKZ14

Please complete this form and send to: **Who Do You Think You Are? Magazine, PO Box 279, Sittingbourne, Kent ME9 8DF**

☑ I would like to subscribe to *Who Do You Think You Are? Magazine* by Direct Debit and receive my first 5 issues for £5* **BEST BUY**

After your trial period your payments will continue at £38.90 every 13 issues, saving 40% on the shop price.

Instructions to your Bank or Building Society to pay by Direct Debit

To: the Manager (Bank/Building Society)

Address

Postcode

Name(s) of account holder(s)

Bank/Building Society account number

Branch sort code

Reference number (internal use only)

Originator's identification number: 7 1 0 6 4 4

Instructions to bank: Please pay Immediate Media Co Bristol Ltd Direct Debits from the account detailed in this instruction subject to the safeguards assured by the Direct Debit Guarantee. I understand that this instruction may remain with Immediate Media Co Bristol Ltd and, if so, details will be passed electronically to my Bank/Building Society.

Signature

Date / /

Banks and Building Societies may not accept Direct Debit mandates from some types of account

YOUR DETAILS (ESSENTIAL)

Title | First name | Surname

Address

Postcode | Country

Home tel. no. | Mobile tel. no.**

Email address**

OTHER PAYMENT METHODS

☐ **UK cheque/credit card** at just £45.40 for 13 issues **SAVE 30%**
☐ **Europe** at £65 for 13 issues   ☐ **Rest of World** at £75 for 13 issues
☐ I enclose a cheque/postal order made payable to Immediate Media Co Bristol Ltd for £_____

Card number

Valid from | Expiry date | Issue number

Signature | Date / /

Immediate Media Company Limited (Publishers of *Who Do You Think You Are? Magazine*) would love to keep you informed by post or telephone of special offers and promotions from the Immediate Media Company Group. Please tick if you'd prefer not to receive these ☐
** Please enter this information so that *Who Do You Think You Are? Magazine* may keep you informed of newsletters, special offers and other promotions by email or text message. You may unsubscribe from these at any time.

Offer ends 31 December 2014

*5 issues for £5 only available to UK residents paying by Direct Debit. After your trial period, your payments will continue at £38.90 every 13 issues, saving 40% on the shop price. If you cancel within two weeks of receiving your fourth issue you will pay no more than £5. Your subscription will start with the next available issue.

3 EASY WAYS TO ORDER

ONLINE AT: www.buysubscriptions.com/whodoyouthinkyouare
PROMOTIONAL CODE **WDBKZ14**

POST: *Who Do You Think You Are? Magazine*, FREEPOST LON 16059, Sittingbourne, Kent ME9 8DF

TELEPHONE: 0844 844 0939†
PLEASE QUOTE **WDBKZ14** WHEN YOU ORDER

YOUR SPECIAL SUBSCRIPTION OFFER:

✓ Try your first **5 issues for just £5**

✓ **Continue to save 40%** on the shop price after your trial period

✓ Benefit from **free additional web content** each month

✓ Receive **FREE UK delivery** direct to your door

✓ **Never miss an issue** of the UK's best-selling family history magazine

HURRY! OFFER ENDS 31 DECEMBER 2014

5 ISSUES FOR £5*

When you subscribe to *Who Do You Think You Are? Magazine* by Direct Debit

~~£24.95~~
SUBSCRIBERS PAY JUST £5*

Subscribe online
www.buysubscriptions.com/whodoyouthinkyouare
Or call our hotline on **0844 844 0939**†

PLEASE QUOTE **WDBKZ14**

†Calls to this number from a BT landline will cost no more than 5p per minute. Calls from mobiles and other providers may vary. Lines are open 8am-8pm weekdays & 9am-1pm Saturday.

DIRECTORY

Selected online resources to help you in your research

▼ GENERAL

Subscription services
www.ancestry.co.uk
www.findmypast.co.uk
www.genesreunited.co.uk
www.thegenealogist.co.uk
The four biggest subscription sites, all of which offer birth, marriage and death indexes, England and Wales censuses (1841-1911) plus lots more.
www.origins.net
www.familyrelatives.com
These subscription sites are also worth checking out for some lesser-known resources including, on Origins.net, the National Wills Index.

The National Archives
www.nationalarchives.gov.uk
Britain's main records archive also houses the London Family History Centre collection. Search holdings online via Discovery and locate other archives using ARCHON.

General Register Offices
www.gro.gov.uk/gro/content/certificates/default.asp
www.groireland.ie
www.nidirect.gov.uk
Copies of birth, marriage and death certificates may be ordered from here.

ScotlandsPeople
www.scotlandspeople.gov.uk

DeceasedOnline.com is an invaluable online resource

Virtual access to the holdings of Scotland's General Register Office.

National Records of Scotland
www.nrscotland.gov.uk
A new organisation combining the National Archives of Scotland and the General Register Office for Scotland.

Public Record Office of Northern Ireland
www.proni.gov.uk
Visit the website to check out the records held here.

The National Archives of Ireland
www.nationalarchives.ie
Houses Irish records, plus search 1901 and 1911 Irish censuses online.

UKBMD.org.uk
www.ukbmd.org.uk
Local birth, marriage and death indexes of England and Wales.

British History Online
www.british-history.ac.uk
Searchable digital library containing some of the core printed sources for the medieval and modern history of the British Isles.

Deceased Online
www.deceasedonline.com
A central database for statutory UK burials and cremations.

British Library Newspapers
www.britishnewspaperarchive.co.uk
A partnership between the British Library and brightsolid online publishing to digitise the British Library's vast collection of newspapers.

Federation of Family History Societies
www.ffhs.org.uk
Join a family history society (FHS) to benefit from expert advice and access to records.

Institute of Heraldic and Genealogical Studies
www.ihgs.ac.uk

The institute runs courses for family historians and has an extensive library.

FamilySearch
www.familysearch.org
Includes billions of names across hundreds of collections – including parish records, censuses, pedigrees and more.

The National Library of Wales
www.llgc.org.uk
The main family history centre for Wales.

Society of Genealogists
www.sog.org.uk
The library of the Society of Genealogists contains many and varied records from all over the world, from census records to transcripts of many monumental inscriptions.

▼ LONDON

1864 and 1868 London Maps
http://london1868.com and
http://london1864.com
Interactive maps showing all the proposed Metropolitan Railways and improvements.

AIM25 - Archives in London and the M25 area
www.aim25.ac.uk
Descriptions of the archives of over 100 higher education institutions, learned societies, cultural organisations and livery companies within the Greater London area.

The Dictionary of Victorian London
www.victorianlondon.org/index1.htm
Contains many out-of-copyright books and assorted illustrations.

Locating London's Past
www.locatinglondon.org
Access to many digital resources relating to early-modern and 18th-century London.

DIRECTORY
ONLINE RESOURCE

London Lives
www.londonlives.org
1680-1800, 240,000 manuscripts from eight archives and 15 data sets, giving access to 3.35 million names.

London Street Name Changes
www.maps.thehunthouse.net/Streets/Street_Name_Changes.htm
Lists of the street name changes that took place in London between two periods: 1857-1929 and 1929-1945.

Museum of London Picture Library
www.museumoflondonimages.com
Over 35,000 images illustrating the history of London and the life of its people from prehistoric times to the present.

Old Bailey Sessions Proceedings
www.oldbaileyonline.org
197,745 criminal trials held at London's central criminal court offer the names of defendants, victims and witnesses.

▼ SCOTLAND

Lothian Health Services Archive
www.lhsa.lib.ed.ac.uk/collections
Material on patients (covered by the Data Protection Act 1998) and doctors and nurses.

Royal Commission on the Ancient and Historical Monuments of Scotland
www.rcahms.gov.uk
Collections of drawings, photos, maps, manuscript material, records of machinery and aerial photographs.

Scottish Archive Network
www.scan.org.uk
Provides a single electronic catalogue of the holdings of more than 50 Scottish archives.

School of Scottish Studies Archives
www.celtscot.ed.ac.uk/archives
A unique collection of material relating to oral and musical traditions, folklore and folksong, old methods of farming and fishing, ways of life and place names.

ScotlandsPeople Centre
www.scotlandspeoplehub.gov.uk
Visit the ScotlandsPeople Centre where you

Could Scotland's national collection of buildings, archaeology and industry help you?

can access digital records all day for just £15. Staff are on hand to assist.

Scottish Catholic Archives
www.scottishcatholicarchives.org.uk
The archive holds material invaluable for Catholic family history.

Scottish Genealogy
www.scotsgenealogy.com
The library holds microfilm copies of all Scottish parish registers, census returns and monumental inscriptions.

Scottish Life Archive
www.nms.ac.uk/our_collections/scottish_life_archive.aspx
Documents and illustrations of Scottish social life in all communities.

▼ WALES

Archives Wales
www.archivesnetworkwales.info
Locate a record office and search the holdings of 21 Welsh archives.

Association of Family History Societies of Wales
www.fhswales.org.uk
Co-ordinates and supports the activities of the Family History Societies in Wales.

National Museum Wales
www.museumwales.ac.uk
A hub for the museums of Wales, including the Rhagor web-site of Welsh national collections and the stories behind them.

▼ IRELAND

Association of Professional Genealogists in Ireland
www.apgi.ie
Members of the association are drawn from every part of Ireland and represent a wide variety of interests and expertise.

Genealogical Society of Ireland
www.familyhistory.ie
The society organises open meetings, lectures, workshops and publishes genealogical material including an annual journal.

Irish Jewish Museum
www.jewishireland.org/irish-jewish-history/museum/
Located in a former synagogue, this museum is home to the Irish Jewish Genealogical Society and Family History Centre.

The National Photographic Archive
www.nli.ie/en/national-photographic-archive.aspx
For images of your ancestors' area, go to the National Library's collection of 630,000 photographs of historic people and places.

▼ INDIA

British Library India Office
www.bl.uk/catalogues/iofhs.shtml
India Office records, including military ones.

The Families in British India Society
www.fibis.org
The Families in British India Society online search of baptism and other records.

▼ PARISH RECORDS

Online Parish Clerks
www.onlineparishclerks.org.uk
Place inquiries about records of a particular parish, and view many collections online.

Parish record collections
www.parishregister.com
(for Docklands ancestors)
www.durhamrecordsonline.com
(for Durham ancestors)
http://seax.essexcc.gov.uk
(for Essex ancestors)

▼ SPECIALIST ARCHIVES

The Commonwealth War Graves Commission
www.cwgc.org

DIRECTORY
ONLINE RESOURCE

Museums, such as the National Maritime Museum at Greenwich, hold collections of records

▷ The Commission records all Commonwealth war dead from the First and Second World War so you can locate their grave or memorial and, frequently, details of their next of kin.

Forces War Records
www.forces-war-records.co.uk
A mixture of military databases.

The London Gazette
www.london-gazette.co.uk/search
The Government's own newspaper has been published daily since 1665, reporting on appointments and promotions of army officers and medal awards.

London museums of health and medicine
www.medicalmuseums.org
The websites of London-based museums with archives relating to the medical profession, including the Royal Pharmaceutical Society, the Royal College of Surgeons and the Worshipful Society of Apothecaries of London.

Marks and Spencer company archive
www.marksintime.marksandspencer.com/the-collection
Find photographs, staff handbooks, uniforms and staff magazines here, although there are few records of individuals. Any surviving are closed for 75 years after creation except to the person concerned or a direct descendant.

Medieval Soldiers
www.icmacentre.ac.uk/soldier/database
Compiled from rolls held at TNA of soldiers serving between 1369 and 1453, mainly during the 100 Years War with France, but including soldiers who served with the English Armies against Scotland.

Modern Records Centre
www2.warwick.ac.uk/services/library/mrc

Find TUC (Trades Union Congress) archives from 1868 onwards. Individual unions represented include the Transport and General Workers' Union and the National Union of Railwaymen. There are also records relating to the motor industry.

Museum of English Rural Life
www.reading.ac.uk/merl
A major archive holding records of big agricultural firms, co-operatives and small farmers alike. Includes company accounts, journals of farm workers, year books, farm diaries, stock books, administrative records, photographs and film.

The National Army Museum
www.nam.ac.uk
This site contains a growing number of short Regimental Histories and guides to researching soldiers from 1660 onwards.

National Coal Mining Museum
www.ncm.org.uk/collections/library
Information on individual pits, mining disasters, unions, 19th-century journals and social conditions for miners.

National Maritime Museum
www.rmg.co.uk/national-maritime-museum
Manuscripts and books relating to naval and merchant shipping are held here, including records of some shipbuilders and repairers, ship owners, barge companies and marine engineers.

The Ogilby Trust
www.armymuseums.org.uk
The trust contains information on all corps and regimental museums in the UK, including contact details and website links.

Royal Mail Archive
www.postalheritage.org.uk/page/archive
This archive holds records for Post Office staff, including minute books with details of appointments, and dismissals and pension records with a summary of a person's working life and the jobs they did within the Post Office from 1860 to 1959.

Scottish Business Archives
www.gla.ac.uk/services/archives/collections/business
Holdings that cover the whole of Scotland and include records of the whisky industry, shipping companies, shipbuilding and repairs, Scottish railways and the textile industry can be found here. Most are from the 19th and 20th century, but a few are from earlier.

Theatre and performance archives
www.vam.ac.uk/content/articles/t/archives-theatre-performance
Part of the V&A Museum in London, the archives include those of individual theatres, photographs, actors and directors, and theatre and dance companies.

Unilever archives
www.unilever.com/aboutus/ourhistory/unilever_archives
Includes staff magazines with obituaries, marriages and long service awards, and detailed card indexes about some Lever Brothers employees in a co-partnership scheme. Colman's, Wall's and Lipton's all feature, as well as original documents, photos and films.

Waterways archive
www.nwm.org.uk
Archives of British Waterways and the early canal companies are held here, with the Manchester Ship Canal and the Weaver Navigation Trust also represented. There are photos, accounts, letters and boat-building plans.

WW2 service records
www.veterans-uk.info/service_records/service_records.html
Download a form to order Second World War service records.

▶▶▶ And best of all, make sure you regularly visit www.whodoyouthinkyouaremagazine.com for expert advice and the chance to share top tips with fellow family historians.